Praise for *A Ca*

"*A Call for Courage* is the book we
prophetic, and yet very practical. Do
and love in these increasingly difficult times? Then get this book and apply what you'll learn to your life!"

—Joel Richardson, *New York Times* bestselling author, speaker, and filmmaker

"If you're only going to read one book this year, read *A Call for Courage.* This is especially true if you are a church leader. I've known Michael Anthony for over twenty-five years, and can attest that he passionately embodies the message of this book. He's not merely courageous; he's fearless because he fears God more than people. I don't know anyone more qualified to write a book that will help believers stand strong in our age of intolerance and fear. With this book, Michael Anthony has given the church a great gift!"

—Keith R. Krell, PhD, DMin, professor of Biblical Exposition, Moody Bible Institute

"This book is a call to personal revival, to confess and forsake any known sin and any doubtful habit. It is also a call to obey God in both the private and public moments of our life. It reminds us that religious freedom is a great gift of God, and that all of us are to be stewards of this great gift to live out God's calling. I pray that this book blesses many."

—Dr. Bill Thrasher, professor and program head of Spiritual Formation and Discipleship, Moody Theological Seminary

"In a world where millions are literally perishing for lack of knowledge, Michael Anthony's *A Call For Courage* is a practical 'how to' salt-and-light manual in the darkness, a courageous and truthful journal on reversing the curse by faith with God's agape love—a must-read!"

—Alveda King, evangelist, civilrightsfortheunborn.com

"My brother and friend in Christ has written a clear and urgent call for believers the world over to engage. Michael Anthony's *A Call For Courage* provides a practical explanation about the state of our nation and world—and why now is the time to step up! This book is informative, thought provoking, and will help you banish fear, replace it with courage, and engage!"

—Gary Frazier, PhD, founder and president, Discovery Missions International

"Outstanding! Michael Anthony will inspire you to live with courage in your personal life and family. *A Call for Courage* will help you address the real issues facing America at this key time—issues that many people are either too afraid to face or don't know where to begin. I highly recommend *A Call for Courage*!"

—Dimas Salaberrios, author of *Street God*, president of Concerts of Prayer Greater NYC

"Here is a missing piece if you struggle to live for the Savior. Want to step up your game? Read *A Call for Courage*. . . . From his teaching and exhortation, he motivates us to enter the conversations happening around us and represent Christ with thoughtful, effective interchange. Be ready to be uplifted. I highly recommend it."

—Bruce W. Fong, PhD, dean, Dallas Theological Seminary, Houston Campus

"*A Call for Courage* is a timely challenge to prepare and inspire the church in the face of increasing hostility to the truths—and people—of God. . . . Michael Anthony admonishes us to meet hate with humility and opposition with love; to meet attacks against our constitutional freedom with unified insistence for our freedom. We dare not do otherwise. The stakes are too high."

—Kelvin Smith, senior pastor, Steele Creek Church of Charlotte; author of *Living on Target*

"Michael Anthony's *A Call For Courage* is a defibrillator to the heart of the church; a must-read for every pastor and Christian leader who wants to see people wake up, step out, and live as the salt and light Jesus called us to be. This book effectively outlines and communicates the battle plan for engaging our culture with the moral issues of our day. It is a call to every believer to step out of the bleachers and into the action, to move from mere spectators to participators in God's rescue mission for humanity, his redemptive plan for the world."

—Matt McGarity, founding and lead pastor, Relevant Church

"Michael Anthony's *A Call For Courage* gives Christians a vision for what their lives should look like in the face of a changing landscape. Thoughtful and practical, this book will inspire and call every reader to a deeper level of commitment and bravery."

—Jonathan Pitts, executive director, The Urban Alternative

"Michael Anthony's *A Call for Courage* comes at a time when I believe we as so-called believers certainly need a spiritual shot in the arm, a kick in the butt, and surely a spiritual awakening! Every one of us needs to read this book! . . . Thank you, Pastor Mike, for that courageous humility you have learned to master, and by sharing it with us in this masterpiece."

—Bill Kerney, senior pastor, Covenant Family Ministries; president, The Black Ministers' Association, York, Pennsylvania

"Michael Anthony has done a great service in calling believers in the Risen Christ to humbly and boldly speak out for the truth. For too long, many Christians have remained quiet or passive in the face of opponents. We need humble courage to counter and communicate with intolerant enemies of biblical truth. He has practical suggestions as to how to carry out our responsibility in this area. He is forceful, clear, and easy to read. Chapter summaries have applications that are very helpful."

—Dr. C. Fred Dickason, former chair of Theology, Moody Bible Institute; professor emeritus of Theology, Moody Bible Institute

A CALL FOR COURAGE

LIVING WITH POWER, TRUTH, AND LOVE IN AN AGE OF INTOLERANCE AND FEAR

MICHAEL ANTHONY

NELSON BOOKS
An Imprint of Thomas Nelson

Published in Nashville, Tennessee, by Nelson Books, an imprint of Thomas Nelson. Nelson Books and Thomas Nelson are registered trademarks of HarperCollins Christian Publishing, Inc.

The author is represented by Alive Literary Agency, 7680 Goddard Street, Suite 200, Colorado Springs, Colorado 80920. www.aliveliterary.com.

Thomas Nelson titles may be purchased in bulk for educational, business, fund-raising, or sales promotional use. For information, please e-mail SpecialMarkets@ThomasNelson.com.

ISBN 978–0–718074135 (e-book)
ISBN 978-0-7180-7415-9 (audio)
ISBN 978-0-7180-9094-4 (HC)

Library of Congress Cataloging-in-Publication Data

Names: Anthony, Michael , 1964- author.
Title: A call for courage : living with power, truth, and love in an age of intolerance and fear / Michael Anthony.
Description: Nashville : Thomas Nelson, 2018.
Identifiers: LCCN 2017020088 | ISBN 9780718090944
Subjects: LCSH: Spirituality--Christianity. | Spiritual life--Christianity. | Christian life.
Classification: LCC BV4501.3 .A56 2018 | DDC 241/.4--dc23 LC record available at https://lccn.loc.gov/2017020088

The Living and True God: Thank you for your indescribable love, for saving me from an empty way of life, and for continually reaching out to me—even when I was incapable, or unwilling, to help myself.

Janet: My dove, you are a bigger blessing than I ever could have dreamed up—hotter, smarter, and wiser than I deserve. You have positively, indelibly, impacted my life, speaking, writing, and ministry. God is gracious, and he continually shows me his grace through you.

Titus and Simeon: My sons, this book was written with you in mind, as a labor of love, knowing that the world you are inheriting is an increasingly complex, hostile place where people of faith are being squeezed like olives in a press. You must keep your heads, guard your hearts, and nourish your souls. If you do, you will be able to live with power, truth, and love in an age of intolerance and fear.

Our Prayer Warriors: Here, in your hands, is the fruit of your earnest prayers. Thank you for believing in me, standing with me, and upholding me before the throne of grace as I undertook this monumental task.

Contents

Foreword

Reading has always been a passion of mine. When I was in elementary and middle school, my constant companions were books and balls–baseballs, basketballs, footballs, tennis balls, volleyballs. If it was round and could be used for some type of competitive sport, I liked it. Baseball was my go-to sport, though, and the New York Yankees were my dream team–always were, always will be.

As a kid growing up in New York in the 1950s, Mickey Mantle was my hero. I watched Yankee games constantly, read newspaper articles about his exploits, and even had a scrapbook filled with pictures and clippings about him. In 1964, Mantle wrote a book titled *The Quality of Courage*. It seemed like an odd title for an iconic home run hitter, but then again, courage was one of his defining characteristics. Mantle experienced and played through more injuries than almost any player of his time. His career statistics are staggering but they would have been off the charts if he'd been healthy during his eighteen years on the field. As an avid Mantle fan I was determined to read the book, regardless of the topic.

Even today, more than fifty years later, some of the content of his book comes to mind. Naturally, the passages about his own struggles with pain and self-doubt made the biggest impact. There were moving anecdotes about Jackie Robinson breaking the color barrier in the major leagues, all-star catcher Roy Campanella sustaining a life-altering injury, Red Sox outfielder Jimmy Piersall enduring mental illness, and even one about Mickey's father unsuccessfully battling cancer at a young age. Mantle gave life to the idea of courage through these stories. Through those tales I saw new facets of courage, such as honesty, standing up to one's fears, and overcoming crushing adversities. The book gave me a new window into the meaning of courage and put that quality on my radar.

Little did I know, as an eleven-year-old kid reading that book, that it was patterned after another that had been written by a president a few years earlier. With my family leading the way, I was also a big fan of John F. Kennedy during his brief presidency. After reading the Mantle book I was introduced to Kennedy's award-winning book *Profiles in Courage*, which described eight historical political figures who demonstrated courage in their public life. While much of that book was over my head at the time—I was only twelve years old when I slowly worked through it—the concept of possessing the "courage of my convictions" was a keeper.

In the intervening years I have had the privilege of encountering courage in many forms and many disparate environments. It is one of the qualities that always stops me in my tracks when it emerges, regardless of the individual or setting involved. Courage is a quality that distinguishes those who make a lasting difference in peoples' lives. The practical application of courage makes the courage-bearer an unforgettable person.

The centrality of courage was highlighted for me once again during my years in graduate school. During that time Jesus Christ transitioned from being a distant, cartoonish hero to a living, life-changing Man of Courage to me. As I became more personally acquainted with Christ and the Word of God, the courage of Jesus was a major revelation. His courage was so provocatively and plainly conveyed in the Bible, showing his thoughts and deeds amid so many life-threatening and world-changing events. His example was undeniable, challenging, and inspiring.

And that is one of the many reasons why Michael Anthony's book about courage is so valuable. The daily question for every person of faith is "how do I translate the incredible courage, perseverance, wisdom, gentleness, and humility of Christ into my own interactions and decisions?" *A Call for Courage* provides some of the practical assistance we need to do that.

Drawing on his own experiences as a leader of people and a servant of Christ, Michael shares about the importance of refusing to settle for what's easy instead of fighting for what is right and desirable. This made an impression on me because of my research indicating that most Christians in America settle for less than the best that God has for them. We settle for unbiblical sermons and predictable religious events. We settle for half-truths and unbiblical worldviews. We settle for a relatively mundane life rather than the transformed life Christ offers us. Shame on us! Perhaps Michael's words will inspire us to reconsider our standards and practices.

Michael guides us to the realization that the problems facing American culture are rarely because of "them" but rather more often because of you and me. Conditions will improve when you and I have the courage to face our own issues and deal with them appropriately. Rather than point our fingers at others and criticize what they think and do, we must identify our responsibility for facilitating positive change. Instead of waiting for others to solve the problems we face, we must figure out how God has prepared us to rise up with his strength, wisdom, and courage to be Christlike in such a time as this.

Would the world be a different place if every follower of Jesus were imitating the mind and heart of the Master? Of course! But it takes courage to do so. The world would be unrecognizable in comparison to the state of affairs we see around us today.

A recent survey I conducted revealed that most Americans do not really believe they are sinners because they do not really believe in the existence of sin. Further, the study found that only 1 percent of Americans believe that when they die they will face some type of eternal penalty for their earthly choices. We have become a nation of self-sufficient individuals who dismiss the idea that God will judge us. (In fact, one of the greatest fears of Americans these days is to be labeled judgmental.) Our feelings aside though, sin exists and we are all guilty of it. When Michael admonishes us to have the courage to acknowledge and repent of our sins, it's a big, countercultural invitation that we need to take seriously.

A Call for Courage is a book for the times. It interacts with the conditions of the day, and relates to the opportunities that each of us have to be people whose courage redefines us, personally, and renews the world around us. Courage is not as widespread as we might think–and certainly less common than it needs to be. Are you willing to be a person of courage? Do you want your life to matter? Is having a lasting, positive legacy a matter of importance to you? Are you willing to be a "fool for Christ" in order to bring about his kingdom? Like the men of Issachar, leaders in Israel a long time ago, will you invest yourself in understanding the times and knowing what to do to foster cultural transformation, even if it is uncomfortable for you? Courage is central to all of these outcomes. Michael's book will help you increase your courage quotient–and that will help you to be the agent of love and change that God has called you to be.

George Barna
Ventura, California
November 2017

Introduction

> If you do what you're supposed to do,
> when you're supposed to do it, the day
> will come when you can do what you
> want to do when you want to do it.
>
> —ZIG ZIGLAR

In my office, I have an autographed photo of Zig Ziglar, the father of motivational speaking. Nearby is a small printout of the above quote. I hope it encourages you as much as it does me.

I often recite Zig's piece of motivational wisdom to my boys in an effort to help them understand the value of living prepared lives. I often recite it to myself as well. I've found Zig's words to be true not only in regard to goal-setting and achievement, but also as they apply to living for God in an increasingly dark, difficult world.

When you live for God in secret, he can make great moves through you in public. There is a direct relationship between how passionate we are for God when no one sees what we're doing and our ability to influence others for him when all eyes are upon us. Don't make the mistake of separating the two. If you make God the love of your life, he will be the fire in your furnace when your day of testing comes. He will orchestrate opportunities to represent him in ways you cannot imagine, because no one, no matter his or her gifts, talents, education, or wealth, can do what only becomes possible when someone is fully yielded to God. A prepared, yielded life is a *ready* life, a courageous life—ready to face fierce opposition at any moment, even in the times we least expect it. A surrendered life is the kind of life that stands up and speaks out while people everywhere are being told to sit down and shut up.

Our society is stewing in a cauldron of moral, racial, financial, political, and theological nonsense. The heat is on, and it's getting turned up. With lightning speed and intensity, growing multitudes of people are mistaking relativism for truth, tolerance for love, fatalism for faith, and mere Bible knowledge for the application of biblical truth. This cocktail is toxic, creating a wake of destroyed lives that think they have progressed. The exact opposite is true. And if people don't begin to stand up and speak out soon—with consistent, humble ferocity—lives will be forever destroyed, not liberated.

The cancers of relativism, fatalism, fear, and tolerance are metastasizing throughout America. The prognosis for a society and nation that do not reverse this course is not delightful. It is deadly. It's time you and I arise and face the challenges facing us, while we still have time. Our readiness to rightly respond with truth, tact, wisdom, love, and courageous humility will determine what takes place in our personal lives, families, neighborhoods, and nation. It's time for courageous humility to arise, because without it, we will surely be overcome.

People who embrace Judeo-Christian values are being tested relentlessly these days, with increasing intensity all around the world. The onslaught is so severe that today's examples quickly become yesterday's news, replaced by fresh instances of hatred toward biblical standards. Millennia-old, commonsense meanings of words are being challenged and changed, with nonsense replacing common sense—all to make room for people demanding a more "tolerant," "inclusive," "loving" culture. In reality, these proponents are hypocrites, doing the very things they accuse others of. They are masters at what I call "reverse intolerance."

Many in leadership positions are ill equipped to educate and train their people about the onslaught against biblical values. Others, distracted by lesser things, have little time or interest to address what matters most. Many are frustrated because we know we should do *something* to turn things around, but we simply don't know where to start.

How in the world do we prepare for and respond to the trials and misunderstandings that have become the new normal in America and throughout the world? The time to prepare for an exam is well before the papers are distributed in class. If "life is school," then the very fabric of society is being tested. This is a test we cannot afford to fail.

I wrote the first draft of this book while holed up in a remote Pennsylvania cabin. I had already made arrangements to sequester myself and write a book—without an agent and without a publisher—convinced that God led me to the endeavor. Two weeks after I scheduled the trip, on the anniversary of my mother's birthday, I received an unsolicited e-mail from Lisa Jackson, with Alive Literary Agency. We had never before spoken. She inquired, "As you've built out your web site with video, apps, the blog, speaking, and more, I'm curious as to where you might see books fitting into that plan." God was at work. Seventeen days later, I was in the cabin, serving as a male midwife for the first draft of the book you're now reading.

After six days of writing, my muscles and joints ached from the exhausting sessions of sitting in a chair, hammering away on my laptop, beating it into submission. My fingers, begging for a break, frequently cramped up during the process. George Orwell said,

"Writing a book is a horrible, exhausting struggle, like a long bout with some painful illness. One would never undertake such a thing if one were not driven on by some demon whom one can neither resist nor understand."[1] In my case, I wasn't driven by a demon, but by a burning passion for what is happening in America and around the world.

This book comes from a deep burden for people of faith and for freedom-loving people everywhere. It comes from a deep passion to help you, the reader, live with power, truth, and love in an age of intolerance and fear.

Our nation and world may be facing our midterms or our final exams. History, in hindsight, will tell. Only men, women, boys, and girls of humble courage can reverse our course, stop evil in its tracks, and win the day. The good news is that humble courage can be developed. It can be developed in *you*.

Do not underestimate the power you have to change the direction of your family, your church, your community, and even your nation. Do not underestimate your ability to be God's agent of change. History is filled with examples of ordinary people just like you—people who did extraordinary things when they found the courage to do what was right in the face of tremendous wrong. What you're about to read will help you develop this courage. And as you develop it, God will begin to write history through *you*.

Michael Anthony
Spring 2018

1

Blinders

"Tell me, when did doilies and your mother's dishes become so important to you?"

—GANDALF THE GREY, *THE HOBBIT*

My family and I were in Colonial Williamsburg taking in the sights, sounds, and tastes it alone offers.[1] We toured the Governor's Palace and the Bruton Parish Episcopal Church, where George Washington, Thomas Jefferson, James Madison, George Whitefield, and others worshipped and served in days long gone. What an awe-inspiring experience it was to contemplate not only those who frequented that hallowed ground but also the topics addressed within its walls. No doubt the pulpit lit fires in the pews—and beyond. The people processed the news of the day through the lens of the Bible, doing so in the streets, around dining tables, in shops, and in taverns. Lives and culture were forged in the process.

As we left the building, the afterglow of amazement radiating in our souls, we rounded the corner and saw a horse-drawn carriage just ahead. I knew our sons, Titus and Simeon, then ages twelve and ten, would love to ride in a carriage like that. And suddenly we were surrounded by a cache of horses and carriages of different colors, shapes, and sizes.

"Wow!" gushed Simeon. "Look at those horses!"

Before you could crack a whip, there we were, caressing them, marveling at their muscles. "Wouldn't it be *so cool* to have a horse, Dad?" he asked.

While Janet and our boys fixed their eyes on the horses' manes and sculpted bodies and the beauty of the carriage, my eyes focused on the contraptions affixed to their heads. Though we were standing at their sides, these steeds could not see us. They were wearing blinders, which limit a horse's focus to only what's right in front of its nose.

When first affixed to its head, a horse resolutely resists blinders. Eventually resistance gives way to acceptance, and the animal embraces a new, subdued way of life, forgetting the freedom it once enjoyed. Many of us—a great majority of us—are going through life as if someone has placed a set of blinders over our eyes. Like restrained, passive, submissive animals, we seem to be incapable of seeing things that are right under our noses. We either can't see them, choose not to see them, or no longer care.

We who embrace Judeo-Christian values have been living as if someone affixed us with a custom set of blinders. In truth, no one did that to us. We've done it to ourselves. The majority of us are now either incapable of seeing what is happening all around us—or have grown resolutely indifferent to our decline. We don't seem to give a d—.

Some of us may care more about my near use of a cuss word in that last sentence than the ways in which we are living life, with more lukewarmth toward God than any person of faith should be comfortable with. Yet comfortably lukewarm is exactly what many of us have become. Jesus said, "Because you are lukewarm—neither hot nor cold—I am about to spit you out of my mouth" (Rev. 3:16). Lukewarm faith is not just a nuisance for Jesus. It is deeply repulsive.

We "traditional values" people may squirm and complain at what's happening around us, just like the horse does when its blinders are first affixed. But then, *exactly like the horse*, we give in and accept a new form of life that is a pale reflection of its former beauty. We've tamed Christianity down to its near irrelevance in America. Our tempered approach to Christian living is not something God can use. It is, in fact, useless.

Shouldn't we be weary of the talking heads on radio, television, and all forms of media (pulpits too) who simply rail against society's woes? All they do is stir the pot. Talk is not just cheap. It is a sin, because when all we do is talk, we are behaving as professional gossips. We end up being good for nothing. We think that merely discussing a problem is the same as seeking to solve it. It isn't.

Many have become disillusioned by how we Christians behave. They don't see us as living sacrifices but as walking hypocrisies.[2] In many ways, they see our lives with an honesty we do not. We say we love Jesus and have been dramatically impacted by his life and teachings—but our lives don't look nearly as dedicated as those who comprised the early church, through whom God set the world ablaze. Far and wide, our lives look remarkably like those of the lost souls we say need to be transformed by the power of God. In some cases, our lives look far worse.

Ravished by postmodernity, where the very concept of absolute truth is questioned or outright rejected, skepticism and cynicism abound over the suggestion that God has revealed himself and his plan through the Bible. Moral "absolutes" are now seen only as personal convictions, lifestyle choices that no one should be concerned with other than the person embracing them (i.e., "If it feels good, do it."). An increasing majority of people don't feel the need to embrace historic, biblical teaching as relevant or valuable to their current, or eternal, well-being. This is true not merely among the unchurched, but also among those who grew up in Bible-respecting homes.

On the more extreme end of the spectrum, there seems to be a growing number of people who are overtly hostile to Christians, Christianity, and historic Judeo-Christian values. They are bent on following *anything* other than the teachings of the Bible, since they feel Christianity has failed not only them but also many in America. They are passionate to take as many people along for their ride as they possibly can, by almost any means possible.

Meanwhile, our church leaders have mistaken speed, size, and numbers for making disciples who look and live like Jesus. We have allowed religious ritual to masquerade as intimacy with God and as the love for our neighbor that proves the reality of our faith.

Our congregations are divided, mirroring the very polarized society in which we live. We have white churches and black churches, contemporary and conservative services, and on and on and on. Rarely do our churches reflect the kingdom of God gathered around the throne of the Lamb, where one day people from every nation, tribe, people, and language, will worship.[3] Not long after the birth of the civil rights movement, and just two millennia from the manger, we have so very much growing up to do.

The faith founded by the Humble One, who also overturned the tables of the money changers, seems to have lost both its humility and courage. We are arrogant when we should be meek, and timid when we should be bold. Our culture is crumbling under the weight of our wanting. For all these things we must thoroughly repent—or we will perish.

Whatever reasons we may have about why many Americans are turned off, tuned out, disinterested, disillusioned, or hostile toward Christians, Christianity, and historic Judeo-Christian teaching, the one truth that we should all agree upon is that the majority of us are unwilling, or unable, to take a long enough look at our lives to stop us in our tracks and make amends. Our refusal to diagnose the root of our problems keeps the solutions at bay.

All of this should wake us up—all of us. If you're just zipping through this chapter, slow down, think deeply once again (or perhaps for the first time), and prepare to adjust your life, your family, your business, and your house of worship—*significantly*. If alive today, surely Albert Einstein would remind us that "insanity is doing the same thing over and over again, expecting different results." If we keep doing what we've been doing, we'll keep getting what we've been getting. Can't we see our folly?

Our problem is not just what's happening around us; it's what we've allowed to happen *to* us. We have allowed Judeo-Christian teaching, principles, and practices to be seen as the problem, rather than the solution. We have allowed ourselves to settle for religious ritual when all along we could be experiencing mighty movements of the Spirit of God.

Great Awakening—*Now*

While a horse has no say in whether or not it lives with blinders, we do. The primary reason we are undergoing an extreme national makeover—the reason America is burning—is because we have neglected the documents and principles that made us who we were and who we are, which hold the keys to us reaching our greatest potential. Our lifestyles are being deeply impacted by the erosion of biblical, Judeo-Christian values. Consider these sobering facts about what is happening in America:

- Our suicide rate is higher than it's been in thirty years, with a rise of 24 percent from 1999 to 2014 alone.[4]

Despair is on the rise. People are losing their sense of fulfillment, joy, and peace. Our descent seems to validate the prophetic theory of Frances Schaeffer, author of *The God Who Is There* and *Escape from Reason*. Schaeffer wrote and lectured that when a society replaces truth with relativism, and rejects the reality of moral absolutes, it results in futile attempts to live below what he called "the line of despair." Above the line of despair are reason, moral absolutes, purpose, and truth. He argued that a full-fledged embrace of relativism cannot but plunge people into deep despair because life itself cannot be lived apart from the design of our Creator.

Schaeffer was simply communicating absolute truth: deep, lasting joy; peace; and fulfillment can only be experienced when we live within God's design.[5] Is our soaring suicide rate a mid-season reflection of our rejection of biblical, moral absolutes that provide the foundation for meaning and purpose in all of life?

- The war on terror has left most of us fearful, numb, and clamoring for safety at all costs. We have accepted fear as the only way of life—to such a degree that children now are living in an Orwellian "Big Brother" society without even realizing there was once an alternative. A generation is growing up with an entirely different definition and experience of *privacy* than we had as recently as a few years ago. Privacy has become more of a concept than the reality it once was.
- We are in the midst of the worst opioid epidemic in our history. In 2015, nearly as many people died from heroin overdoses as from auto accidents.[6] The surge of suicides and drug use reflects our search for exhilaration and escape from the pains of real life. Freedom and life are giving way to addiction and death.
- The average child is exposed to pornography at the age of eleven—and the age of exposure is getting lower. The porn industry is changing—and ruining—lives. Twelve percent of all websites are pornographic. Twenty percent of men

admit to watching online porn at work. (This does not reflect the number of men who watch porn at work and don't admit it, or the number who watch porn at home in secret.) Thirty-five percent of all Internet downloads are pornographic. There are more than 65 million requests for porn on search engines (25 percent of total requests) daily. More than half of the nearly $5 billion a year made in the porn industry is fueled by American demands.[78]

Requests for labiaplasty have exploded, with a surge of 36 percent in 2016 alone. "'I am asked about labiaplasty at least once a month,' says ob-gyn Jennifer Gunter, MD, who runs a specialty clinic for vulvar conditions at Kaiser Permanente in San Francisco, California. 'Five years ago, I was probably asked one to two times a year.'"[8]

Many attribute this increasingly popular plastic surgery trend to the rise of porn use among men and women in mainstream society. Women want their bodies to look like those they have been viewing in pornographic photos and videos—and so do their men.[9] Healthy views of physiology, sex, and sexuality are rapidly giving way to increasingly distorted, unhealthy, even violent views that objectify men, women, boys, and girls.

- The number of divorces (let alone marriages that subsist out of necessity rather than happiness) paints a sad portrait of monogamy. Forty-one percent of first-time marriages end in divorce, and the percentages get dramatically higher for second and third marriages.[10] Many people have tremendous difficulty communicating, remaining faithful, reconciling, and loving.

Is it a coincidence that we are witnessing these downturns while there is increasing ignorance, disinterest, and even hostility toward both the Bible and the Bible-influenced documents and philosophies that led to America's birth? I don't think so. Today so many mistake mere Bible knowledge for the application of its teachings. (I am not arguing that America was once a "Christian nation." *I've not made that claim—nor will I.* I will say, however, that we are a nation whose people are galloping away from the values that most protect and promote a society marked by God-given liberty and the blessings therein.)

A Different Approach to Truth

We need a "second reformation," a new "great awakening," where the *application* of biblical truth—in light of local, national, and world events—transforms every aspect of our lives. This is not something that needs to begin with other people. It needs to begin with you and me *today.*

To remove our blinders, we must read our Bibles differently than we have, doing so in light of world events—to such a degree that biblical truths are *applied* in relevant, practical, powerful ways. Many Christians only have the most basic understanding of the Bible and the most popular verses, Bible stories, and characters. There are many "Chreasters" (those who only darken church doors on Christmas and Easter) in the United States. They need to dig deeper into God's Word and draw near to God, to really understand his heart, mind, and mission, so his truths can be personally applied and culture can be positively transformed.

But in many other instances, the problem is not that many of us don't know the Word, but that we're not putting into practice the Word we know. We are not bringing the Bible to bear on the issues of the day, in our own lives, families, houses of worship, and nation. Many of us have mistaken knowledge for application. Whether through unwitting ignorance or overt defiance, the outcome is the same: as a consequence, America is hemorrhaging significantly.

If we began to read our Bibles with a keen eye for *immediately and thoroughly applying* its truths personally, in our family lives, and in our leadership roles within our nation, we would see widespread spiritual awakenings of epic proportions, perhaps unlike anything we've ever seen in American history. If we were to study the history of *real* revivals, genuine spiritual awakenings, we would see the common thread of unconditional surrender to an irresistible God. *The price of real revival is paid through real repentance.*

I believe a real movement of repentance across America is exactly what must happen if our country is to move forward into new territory. This is a major reason why I believe the National Week of Repentance (WeekofRepentance.com) is such a vital part of a real American recovery.

One of the ways we remove our blinders, and keep them off, is by reading and rereading American history and the documents that shaped America. Read and often reread all the classics written by our Founding Fathers, beginning with Jefferson, Washington, and Franklin. We need to rediscover, re-embrace, and reteach the Declaration of Independence, the Bill of Rights, and our Constitution, along with the historical contexts in which they were forged—and their importance in guiding and governing us today. These documents, and the worldview that they espouse, form the backbone, soul, fabric, compass, and rudder of what makes America the "land of the free and the home of the brave."

Us, Not "Them"

I was at a gathering of heavy-hitting Christian leaders the year of the 2016 American presidential election. More than one hundred leaders were there, each concerned about the state of America and the upcoming election. During the gathering, a leader took the time to show a brief video that put out a call for revival in America. The scriptures highlighted in the video are perhaps the most frequently referenced verses when Christians bring up the subject of revival. They are 2 Chronicles 7:13–14:

> When I shut up the heavens so that there is no rain, or command locusts to devour the land or send a plague among my people, if my people, who are called by my name, will humble themselves and pray and seek my face and turn from their wicked ways, then I will hear from heaven, and I will forgive their sin and will heal their land.

When the video ended, the presenter put out a sincere plea for intercession on behalf of America. As I looked around the room, I could see heads nodding and facial expressions that agreed: We need to intercede for America. America is in trouble. We need to pray for revival.

Who can disagree with a call for intercession? No one, if that person is reading his or her Bible. But there was a problem with the conclusion embraced by the video's presenter—and the conclusion that most people reached by agreeing with his well-meaning, yet misguided, application of 2 Chronicles 7:13–14. For all the buzz about revival these days, I'm convinced we don't have a clue what we're asking for. This is because we have little idea what God is looking for, and where real revival begins. Even when we read the scriptures about revival, it might as well be as if we were trying to read Hebrew or Greek with no education in either.

I hesitated for a moment, unsure if I should say anything to the presenter and the group, especially since everyone seemed to agree with his sincere call for intercession. Then I figured, "Why not? I was invited here, and I have a chance to express myself." I prayed, *Lord, help me to share in a way that is well received, because I believe there are nothing but good intentions behind the misapplication of these powerful verses.*

A few other people made comments, and then the moderator called on me to make mine. I agonized, struggling with how I might say what was on my heart in a way that would not offend, but rather would inspire, both the person making the presentation and everyone in the room.

Eyes closed at first, my right hand raised in a gesture of self-dismissal, I opened my mouth and let these words slip from my lips:

> Please don't misunderstand what I am about to say, and I struggle with whether or not I should even say it. Who am I among such a great group of leaders as this to say *anything*? The video presentation was outstanding, and I'm very thankful it was created.
>
> The only problem is that 2 Chronicles 7:13–14 isn't about *intercession*. It's about *repentance*. It's a call for repentance among God's people—not among people in the world. Despite everything that is happening in our nation, we Christians have still not begun to call out to God the way he says we must before we can expect to see him move in power. What God is calling his people to do—that we have not yet begun to do—is to *repent*.
>
> Second Chronicles 7:14 is an if-then statement. God, in his grace, tells us in advance what he is looking for, and what we can expect from him when we honor him with genuine humility.[11]
>
> Again, thank you so very much for the opportunity to speak, and please do not take my words as anything other than being offered in sincerity, with the utmost respect for everyone here.

The response in the room was palpable. Several quiet cries of "Yes!" arose, and heads began nodding up and down, in unified agreement. Smiles of affirmation came from multiple angles. I knew that the arrow, hesitantly launched and intended not to wound but to heal, had hit its mark.

American Christianity needs to be saved. I think many Christians are more in love with the idea of revival than they are with Jesus, the Author of revival. I much prefer praying for Jesus' return as the answer to all our woes than to limit my prayers by asking him to move for what will be, if we're honest, just a season.

Real change does not begin in the White House. It begins in God's house, among God's people. And if you haven't noticed lately, God's house needs a thorough housecleaning. Our failure to look at ourselves, and to apply the Bible to our own lives—in light of local, national, and world events—is squashing our ability to change. It's hindering the spiritual awakening that needs to begin within each of us.

American Christianity needs to be saved.

It's time we Christians get honest with God, get honest with one another, and rediscover who we are, what we've allowed ourselves to become, and how we have embraced lives of apathy, distraction, and detachment instead of an all-consuming fire for God. Whenever God wants to do a significant work in society, he raises up an individual, and then individuals, to bring that work about. Where are you in God's desire to awaken America?

The "revival" America needs is not "out there." It's right here, among us Christians. If we want to see the world change, we need to see the church change first.

Courageous Humility

While each of us may have our opinions about the biggest problem facing America and the world, our real concern should be not a single problem but the *convergence* of them all, making for what many should be seeing as a perfect storm. Never before have so many people felt such fear and concern over what has happened, and is happening, to our nation.

If you are afraid and concerned, you are not, by a long shot, alone. It seems like every time we turn around, we hear another piece of news that tells us all is not right in America or the world. What can people of faith do, and how should we do it to turn things around before it's too late? How do we prepare ourselves, our families, our houses of worship, and our communities for what we are experiencing, and what looms in the distance and is drawing near?

The chapters that follow are designed to spark a genuine spiritual awakening in your life, family, house of worship, and our nation. Let the words you read drive you to your knees in a newfound pursuit of God, depending on him, rather than yourself, for strength. Let them stimulate conversations in your family, at work, and in your house of worship. Let them help you rise above whatever circumstances you may face, so that you are not overcome, but begin living as an overcomer.

By the time we're done, you will be educated and equipped to such a degree that you'll be empowered to help others do what you will learn to do: stand up and speak out in this day where cowardice and arrogance have run amuck. You will learn how to rise above obstacles with what I call "humble courage"—and you will be able to teach others how to do the same.

Are you ready? Here we go . . .

IN A NUTSHELL

COURAGEOUS HUMILITY IN ACTION

Practical Things You Can Ponder and Practice Right Now

- Have you confused discussing a problem with trying to solve it?

- Have you believed the lie that the real spiritual awakening we need is out there in the hearts and lives of other Christians and unbelievers, that it starts with someone other than you? If so, why not ask God to start the awakening with you?
- We need a "second reformation," a new "great awakening," where the application of biblical truth—in light of local, national, and world events—takes center stage in each of our lives. This needs to start in personal lives, our families, and our churches, beginning with *you*.
- What's holding you back from being completely sold out for Jesus Christ and biblical teaching at this key time in world history?
- Have you mistaken intercession for repentance? Have you been waiting for someone else to be the change God is calling you to be?

2

Courage Matters

> We must always take sides. Neutrality helps the oppressor, never the victim. Silence encourages the tormentor, never the tormented.
>
> —ELIE WIESEL

We were in Hyde Park, London, having made our way to "Speakers' Corner." A group of us were on our way to Israel for a study tour after graduating from seminary a month earlier. Rather than flying directly to Israel, we decided to stop for a few days in England and do some sightseeing en route.

Speakers' Corner is a popular tourist attraction, getting its name from the men and women who gather there and talk about the issues of the day, specifically those two subjects you're never supposed to address in such public settings—politics and religion. Some wear sandwich boards with slogans, while others speak standing on crates, hoping their small stage gives them a bigger platform to persuade people about their cause.

I was particularly curious about the Corner because I had some experience speaking in public spaces. Years earlier, I began preaching on a train station platform in New Jersey.[1] In London, I wanted to see what people were saying and how they were saying it. My friend Natalie[2] and I planned to make a short visit, watch the speakers do their thing, and then grab some fish and chips or maybe some bangers and mash.[3]

Natalie and I circulated among the sparse crowds, stopping briefly near the speakers to hear them talk about the day's headlines or proselytize for converts to whatever faith—or lack thereof—they embraced. No one had a very large crowd except one man who was farthest from us. About twenty-five people encircled him. He was on a wooden crate, was very animated, and clearly had the attention of his listeners.

As an animated Italian, I was drawn to his body language that seemed all too familiar. As we drew closer, we began to make out the man's voice and that of the crowd, which clearly found him entertaining because we could hear their outbursts of laughter in response to his comments. This looked like it would be a chance for free entertainment.

The man was a Muslim, and he was making fun of Christians.[4] The crowd, finding him to be the Corner's best speaker, grew, and so did the laughter. But as others were laughing, Natalie and I were grieving. While the man had reasonable concerns about how some Christian evangelists appear on television, he also made overgeneralizations while comparing his faith and God to ours. (I don't mind at all if someone criticizes Christians or Christianity in respectful, honorable ways. I've had many friendly debates with people about Christ, Christianity, and world religions. When people are respectful, it's always a pleasure to dialogue.) The crowd of twenty-five quickly doubled, and although we were about fifty feet away, we could hear the speaker loud and clear. That audience was about to get even larger, louder—and potentially dangerous.

As the man continued, the crowd's laughter swelled, becoming more frequent as he continued to mercilessly mock Christians and Christianity. Then someone in the back of the pack broke the trend, shouting out, "Yes, but the big difference between what you believe and what I believe is that when you sin, you have no one who has died for the forgiveness of your sins—but I have someone who died for mine and forgives me."

The man on the box immediately stopped. No longer looking down at the crowd from his crate, he looked up, straight into the eyes of the person who had challenged him. In what seemed like staged unison, the heads of everyone in the crowd simultaneously spun around to find the man who had the audacity to contradict the speaker. Like lasers, their eyes hit their mark. *They were staring at me.* Gulp.

Just moments before, my stomach had been growling as I fantasized about fish, chips, and sausages. Debating a Muslim—and a particularly angry one at that—was not on the day's agenda. *How did I get myself into this predicament?* I happened to be at the right place at the right time, courtesy of divine orchestration. God had been preparing me for this exam for quite a while.

The silence was broken when the man cracked another savage joke about his Christian television nemeses and all the heads spun back around, their eyes and ears ready to receive from him once again.

What then developed must have resembled a tennis match. The heads of the crowd shot back and forth as they watched us debate, from the speaker to me, back to the speaker, then to me. This went on for many minutes—feeding the crowd that continued to grow. The speaker became more and more unsettled, and the audience began to mirror his agitation.

The crowd had grown to more than one hundred people, and we were now in the thick of a very hot, yet very substantive debate, in which God enabled me to center on the cross of Jesus Christ and what it means to be a real Christian, regardless of what many may see on "Christian" television. I was totally unprepared for what happened next, but God wasn't. He had prepared Natalie.

I recalled Deuteronomy 18:15–22,[5] which is an important passage about the one-of-a-kind prophet God promised to raise up who would be like, but superior to, Moses—the one who would be Israel's Messiah. In hindsight, we know this to be Jesus of Nazareth, the Christ, God's anointed. The only problem was that I didn't have a Bible on me.

"Do you have a Bible?" I asked Natalie.

"Yes!" she exclaimed, as she reached into her handbag, fishing for the small Bible she kept with her wherever she traveled.

I turned to Deuteronomy 18 and began to read aloud for the man and the crowd.

The man challenged my volley, saying "That's not what it says! You've *changed* it!"

"No, I didn't," I said. "Here, why don't you read it for yourself—and read it to the crowd?" I handed the Bible to the person in front of me, gesturing for him to pass it forward.

As it made its way through the crowd, the Bible bobbed up and down from person to person, eventually finding its way into the speaker's hands where he raised it to his eyes and began to read the passage aloud for all to hear. Midway through reading, however, he stopped, put the Bible down to his side, and changed the subject. It was obvious that he could tell I did not change the passage—and that if he were to continue reading, it would result in his teaching the crowd about the *biblical* Jesus, something his distaste for the faith made him unwilling to do that day as I was debating him.

Charged by the Spirit, I kept pressing the issue, however, keeping the focus on Jesus, the cross, and the exclusivity of peace with God and forgiveness of sin being found only through him. Realizing that the real opportunity lay in addressing the crowd, not merely the speaker, I began directing my comments toward them, now taking full advantage of this divine moment God had thrust me into.

After about forty-five minutes of public debate, it became obvious that the man had been defeated. And he was not happy about it, his haughtiness now mixed with open hostility. The case for Christ had been overwhelming. This man would not—*because he could not*—respond to the strength of argument that was supernaturally (and completely to my amazement) flowing from my mouth. (There are some people who believe God no longer speaks in the same ways in which he once did. But I'm living proof that he still does. In the twenty-second chapter of the book of Numbers, God used an ass to deliver his message. In Speakers' Corner that day, he was using the modern equivalent by speaking through me.)

I asked "Can I have the Bible back?" He motioned for me to approach him, saying "Come!"

My heart began to pound as I took my first steps toward him. The crowd parted as I slowly moved toward the Bible—and the angry man holding it. God gave me the grace to remember that it's often not *what* we say that wins people over but *how* we say it. Arriving at the box he used as a platform to the man's right side, I extended my hand in a gesture of kindness, a conciliatory handshake.

The look on his face revealed that my gesture both perplexed and vexed him. This was not at all what he had expected. My demeanor, completely antithetical to his hatred of my faith and now, it seemed, me, presented a serious problem to his credibility with his once captive crowd. He had lost them. A large part of what he had been railing against was the racism of Christians. Obviously I was not living up to the stereotype he had so passionately portrayed about Christians.

He brushed my hand aside, attempting to again address the crowd and divert them from the fact that he had been defeated. But it was too late. The crowd knew better and saw for themselves that he was not practicing what he was preaching.

The crowd needed to see what it meant for someone to "[speak] the truth in love" (Eph. 4:15) in the face of blatant hostility. I wanted them to see a different kind of Christian from the ones they had been laughing about. This, I believe, is what the whole world needs to see in this dark hour of human history. They need to see real, authentic Christ-followers.

While harboring no anger in my heart toward the speaker, I realized the debate had culminated into a chance to show the crowd that stereotypes are not beneficial, and that adversity need not lead to animosity. But I also wanted to ensure that this man would not return to Speakers' Corner and continue to cause division, leading more people astray.

This isn't just my story. It's *God's* story—and it can be *your* story too—the story of how courage can arise in the midst of unexpected trials, at the exact time it is needed most.

With a kind and respectful tone of voice, I turned and spoke to the crowd. "Let it be known to everyone," I said, as I respectfully held out my hand one last time, "that the man who is condemning racism, criticizing the faith I love and embrace, is rejecting my gesture of peace and kindness by refusing to shake my hand."

With that, I retrieved the Bible and turned to make my way back to Natalie, the crowd now silent. I only walked a few steps before hearing the speaker utter, in a strong but quiet voice, "Somebody *kill* that man!"

Bible in hand, heart in throat, I watched as the crowd again parted in what felt like slow motion. My eyes scanned left and right as I cautiously made my way back to Natalie, wondering if I would make it out of there uninjured, let alone alive. I did, and no one was laughing at Christ or Christians anymore.

I don't remember what we had for lunch that afternoon—I'm sure it was delicious—but I will never forget how God showed up in unexpected power and won the day. He had put me in the right place at the right time to say and do something I never would have ventured to do on my own. Something I never *could* have done on my own.

This isn't just my story. It's *God's* story—and it can be *your* story too—the story of how courage can arise in the midst of unexpected trials, at the exact time it is needed most. It's the story of how God can use all kinds of modern-day donkeys to stand up and speak out in an increasingly sit down, shut up world.

God's Story, Your Story

If you haven't noticed, today's world needs a tremendous, ongoing infusion of courage—the kind of courage mere mortals can't muster. We need the kind of courage made possible by God. This kind of courage is available to you—and to anyone and everyone—and it's absolutely essential if we hope to see our nation and world change.

It's time to stand up and speak out in whatever "Speakers' Corner" God may have placed you. Courageous humility can overcome loud shouting, hatred, and even violence. It's time for humble courage to arise in you, in me, and in a gentle, resolute army of people across this nation and around the world—because a growing army of intolerant haters is rapidly rising and multiplying. If they win, we all lose.

IN A NUTSHELL

COURAGEOUS HUMILITY IN ACTION

Practical Things You Can Ponder and Practice Right Now

- If God can use a donkey, he can use anyone. *He can use you.*
- Do you tend to let your fear of people keep you from doing what's good, noble, necessary, and right?
- Do you need to ask God to forgive you for your silence? Have you let apathy, rather than courage, rule your life? Why not ask God to cultivate courageous humility in you so that it overcomes fear and pride? Ask him to do the same in your family, among your friends, and in your place of worship.
- What kind of story are the actions of your life writing? Is it a tale of fear and trembling, or faith and courage?

3

Heroes and Underdogs

When they see the courage of Peter and John and realized that they were unschooled, ordinary men, they were astonished.

—ACTS 4:13

"Dad," he began, with a puzzled look on his face, "how come when I read the Bible, and compare it to what church looks like, they don't look the same?" My then-twelve-year-old son got it. Why don't we?

If we're really honest with ourselves, and honest with God, we will admit that our lives don't often resemble those of the heroes and underdogs in the Bible. The tragic discrepancies between our lives and those of biblical heroes and underdogs need not be as deep and wide as they have become. In fact, the discrepancies need to be dealt a deathblow. Only then will we be able to tackle relativism, fatalism, and fear. Only then will we be able to address the perfect storm of moral, racial, financial, and theological issues that has converged upon lives, families, and communities, which threatens to squelch the movement of God and undo our nation.

Most of us love to read the stories and hear soaring sermons about the heroes and underdogs of old, those whose exploits are commemorated in the Bible. We love the stories of Samson; Gideon; Ruth; David and Goliath; Elijah on Mt. Carmel; Nehemiah; Esther; Shadrach, Meshach, and Abednego; and Daniel. We get misty-eyed and fired up when reading about the apostles, who, after being sternly commanded to stop teaching about Jesus, upped the ante and boldly cried, "We must obey God rather than human beings!" (Acts 5:17–29).

We Christians love these stories because they are central to our heritage. When we tell these stories, we are sharing part of our glorious past, about how God used ordinary people to accomplish extraordinary feats. But our words and deeds don't often look like the lives of these characters. No matter which Bible translation you embrace, when we read the biblical stories and compare how people lived then to how most American Christians live today, it all seems vastly different. It's almost as if we are reading from the ficticious RSV—the *Reversed* Standard Version.*

Many of us first heard the epic Bible stories in our youth, but then we "matured" just enough to render them and their lessons irrelevant for our hectic, distracted, modern lives where comfort and convenience have replaced trust in God and courage before people. When we hear these stories again, as adults, their lessons are often reduced to mere principles suiting watered-down objectives like how to reduce stress, overcome your business challenges, beat the odds for getting that next promotion, believe God for a

* I'm using "RSV" in a creative way, not at all referring to the Revised Standard Version.

hot spouse, or whatever other applications we may come up with to make sure the Bible fits in with our situations and interests.

We've belittled the Bible. It has become a book about mere mortal success—by whatever definition of *success* one may choose to embrace. We seem to have lost our hunger for God, our spiritual "eye of the tiger," and with it a passion for real success, the outpouring of God's presence that surpasses all other pursuits and pleasures.

Many of us first heard the epic Bible stories in our youth, but then we "matured" just enough to render them and their lessons irrelevant for our hectic, distracted, modern lives where comfort and convenience have replaced trust in God and courage before people.

Moses is a great example of what we should be. He was not content with going into the land God promised without the presence of the landgiver. Just after being told that he and the people of Israel would enter the land "flowing with milk and honey," accompanied by an angel, but not the Lord himself, Moses said: "If your Presence does not go with us, do not send us up from here" (Ex. 33:15).[1]

The timing of Moses' words is noteworthy. It comes *after* he had been meeting with God, face-to-face, as a man meets with a man (Ex. 33:11). He and the seventy elders of Israel had *already* seen God's feet and eaten a meal together with God, the precursor to the Lord's Supper (Ex. 24:10; Matt. 26:17–30). Earlier, Moses had seen God's presence in the pillar of cloud by day and fire by night (Ex. 13:21) and in the miraculous ten plagues God used to set his people free. Moses was in the thick of it when the impossible happened, as he stretched out his hand and the power of the Almighty coursed through his frame: a wall of water formed on his left and his right, and the people walked right through (Ex. 14:21–22). He would forever remember that strange, burning bush that got it all started, the holy ground upon which he stumbled, and the call of God that catapulted him into national leadership and the pages of history.

I don't know about you, but I would be content to have witnessed just one of the things Moses saw. But not Moses, not that servant of the Most High. Instead, each exploit wound up making him more hungry, more curious—and more convinced that the blessings God gives are not equal to the blessing God is. For Moses, God was the goal. God was his success. The greatest of all Old Testament prophets knew that success without God was nothing.

There is a life-changing lesson to be learned from Moses' understanding of success, and we would do well to marinate in it to the point where his understanding becomes ours. Until such time, we are merely toying with success, not hungering for it.

Foreign Passion, Fire at Home

We have grown so accustomed to operating in our own strength and wisdom that we don't realize how weak and vulnerable we've become. Moses' words—and his passion—seem strange to us today. They leave us scratching our heads, not falling on our faces before God, in awestruck dependence. A society that places self at its epicenter, rather than God, has no hope but to create a culture of fearful creatures whose primary pursuits cannot help but sink to mere pleasure and self-preservation. In the end, the people in such a society will have neither.

The great tragedy of the twenty-first century is that the Bible is no longer seen as a book about God. It's become a book about us. The real culture war is not about us. It is about God. It is about finding pleasure in him and pleasing him in the process. When life becomes about people rather than God, then truth, love, and faith are mistaken for—and replaced by—relativism, tolerance, and fatalism. Life becomes an exercise in futility. We become enamored with the things God gives us and lose our fascination and love for God—the only true source of fulfillment.

Do you want more of the doldrums that have become the new norm in America—the division, decline, detachment, and depression? Of course you don't! Remember Moses: he did not allow himself to become content with where he was in his walk with God. He did not find his satisfaction in the things God gave but in the gift of God himself. Moses always wanted more of his Redeemer—and his Redeemer showed himself to have a tireless, bottomless reserve to be tapped into and enjoyed. How much of the presence of God are you hungry to have? Will you set aside lesser things to pursue the greatest and most fulfilling of all pursuits?

Evil is relentless but fragile. It can be crushed by courage.

A good chunk of what it means to pursue God is to adopt a perpetual, growing stance against evil—in all its forms, at all times, starting with your own soul as you fight for the souls of others. In order for light to overcome the darkness, courage is not merely important; it's imperative. Merely being a polite person will do little to stem the torrent of evil. Evil is relentless but fragile. It can be crushed by courage. But what's even more striking is that evil can be crushed by the most ordinary of people—people just like you and me.

Exceptions or Examples?

Extreme views are rarely healthy. They often end up hindering, not helping us, because the majority of life is not lived in the realm of the extreme, but somewhere in between.

In order to demonstrate humble courage, we must identify whether or not we've embraced an extreme view about the Bible and the characters it portrays. We must, because our view of the Bible affects our view of *life*. This, in turn, affects how we go through life. But we need to do more than simply identify the existence of an extreme view. If it exists, we must replace it with one that is correct. A proper view of the Bible will help us successfully navigate through *every* area of life—and will positively impact the very fabric of the society in which we find ourselves blanketed.

Exceptions?

The first extreme view is to conclude that the Bible is primarily a book of *exceptions*. Its stories, therefore, involve superior, nearly perfect people, unique from anyone else who's ever lived or will live. At best, a modern-day, supernatural, world-changing life is only for exceptional people—for people other than us. At worst, such a life is certainly not possible for you. Embracing this view leads to a life that sits you down on the fifty-yard line so you can do nothing more than watch others score goals and touchdowns while you settle for spectatorship.

Examples?

The other extreme view is that the Bible is solely a book of *examples*. Its pages, therefore, depict repeatable miracles that can be initiated by nearly anyone with enough faith and fortitude. This view creates an entirely different set of problems than the first. It sets up proponents for failure any time things don't go as expected. It makes the fundamental mistake of forgetting that there are many times in the Bible where a bit of elbow grease must be coupled with faith when history is to be written. Since faith alone is mistakenly viewed as the primary activating ingredient, the weight of failure cannot help but be placed squarely on the shoulders of whoever didn't have enough of it to make things change.

Which view do you have? Your conclusion will determine everything in your life. It will impact your interest in influencing and your ability to influence the world around you. Think about it before you read any further. What do you believe? Is the Bible a book of exceptions or examples?

The Big Picture

A great majority of us are missing the larger point and purpose of why miracles are recorded in the Bible: we mortals should resist, with every molecule in our being, the notion that God needs perfect, powerful people to bring about change. In order to stand up and speak out when mere mortals are telling you to sit down and shut up, you have to rediscover the truth about God, how he operates, and the kinds of people he uses.

We mortals should resist, with every molecule in our being, the notion that God needs perfect, powerful people to bring about change.

The Bible is a book of exceptions *and* a book of examples, with one game-changing clarification: a major theme of the Bible is that when ordinary people fully surrender to God and make it their ambition to love him with all their heart, mind, strength, and soul (even imperfectly and inconsistently, as we all do), we move from the ordinary to the *extraordinary*. We begin to see God do otherwise unbelievable things through us, things we mere mortals will not—and cannot—do on our own. We *become* courageous and demonstrate courage with supernatural humility. The boredom and frustration of life evaporate, replaced by an excitement and exhilaration that can only come when we fight battles fueled with far more than our own strength.

A person must believe in Someone beyond himself or herself in order to achieve anything beyond belief. We may very well have come to the point in our nation—and in many parts of the world—when a series of genuine miracles is now needed to get us up and out of the moral, racial, and financial quagmires in which we are drowning. The miracles can come if and when we (re)discover how God operates—when we replace our faulty, extreme views of the Bible and how God operates with the truth.

The Bible is not primarily a book of exceptions, though many exceptions are recorded within. It is, rather, meant to be a book of examples of how God uses—how he has always used—super ordinary people to do superhuman things. Embracing this view will positively change everything in your life, and the lives of others around you.

Living a Limitless Life

It's been said, "If you limit what you *will* do, you limit what you *can* do."[2] On one hand, most of us are exactly like the unlikely, incapable, unknown, ordinary people in the Bible. This is great news, because from their feats, we learn that there is hope for us too. But while the heroes and underdogs of the Bible may have been unlikely, incapable, unknown, and ordinary, they were also *willing* to take decisive action in the face of incredible odds and opposition. They were engaged and courageous, rather than distracted and cowardly. You and I need to stop limiting what we *will* do for God, because until we do, we're consciously limiting what we *can* do.

Every hero and underdog of the Bible had something in common that is unfortunately very uncommon today, even among people who claim to be following God: each was fed up with merely going through the motions with their Maker. And each had set their sights on the fulfillment of a vision that was bigger than their own lives and livelihood. They realized that real faith is a partnership of working with God, not an invitation to watch from the sidelines. They became fully yielded to him—surrendered—sometimes even to the point of death, willing to do whatever it took to glorify him. That's when they began to stand up and speak out, and when the world around them began to sit up, take notice, and change. Big change begins on a small scale, with one willing, courageous person at a time. Are you living a surrendered life? What is keeping you from taking the plunge and living a life without limit for the glory of God? Have you in any way limited what you are willing to do for God?

Big change begins on a small scale, with one willing, courageous person at a time. . . . Have you in any way limited what you are willing to do for God?

I believe that one of the main reasons freedom and faith are rapidly diminishing in our culture is that common, ordinary people like you and me have not yet been *willing* to act with unwavering resolve for a purpose that is bigger than our own lives, as biblical characters did. If the apathy and cowardice so prevalent today were the norm during World War II, we'd all be speaking German, Japanese, or Italian—with far more consequences than mere language.

If the attacks on freedom and faith concern you, as they should, then you should be even more concerned about what is happening in our world today, because today's apathy and cowardice are virtually guaranteeing that history will more than merely repeat itself. Unless things turn around—unless ordinary people turn things around—what is happening today will soon make history look like a walk through a Midwestern pasture on a beautiful summer morning.

Apathetic, fear-filled lives—lives that lack courage and are unwilling to stand up and speak out—will ensure a future of dictatorial fascism, oppression, imprisonment, and control such as the world has never before seen. The meek may inherit the earth, but if they don't stand up and speak out, and do it consistently, there won't be much of an inheritance left to enjoy.

> If the apathy and cowardice so prevalent today were the norm during World War II, we'd all be speaking German, Japanese, or Italian—with far more consequences than mere language.

Heroes and underdogs are humble, courageous people who place no limits on what they *will* do for God. They become people who *do* great things for God and for the people around them.

What about you? Have you in any way limited what you are *willing* to do for God? If so, you've already limited what you *can* do. Are you willing to do whatever it takes to see the presence of God become the all-consuming fire of your life, to see the kingdom agenda of God saturate and transform everything you touch? If you are, your capacity to do great things for God—to live a life akin to the heroes and underdogs of the Bible—will abound. Yours will be a life of deep satisfaction, because there is nothing more satisfying than partnering with God.

Think about this long and hard: there are many empires but only one kingdom, the kingdom of God. Empires last for a season, but the kingdom of God endures forever. Which are you building?

If you want God to use you mightily and consistently, you have to be willing to do what others won't. If we think the same old apathetic, cowardly approaches we've been embracing are going to bring about dramatic change in our lives, families, churches, and nation, we are sorely mistaken. What about you? Are you willing to do what others won't?

The Hero in the Mirror

Where are the modern-day "Samsons," people who have roller-coaster, double-minded pasts, who've made big mistakes but have determined to make the most out of whatever remaining time they may have, not at all for themselves, but for the glory of God?

Where are today's "Gideons," the underwhelming minority ready to take on the establishment, defeat the odds, and do humanly impossible things—not for themselves, but for the reputation of God and the advancement of his agenda and kingdom?

Are modern-day "Daniels" anywhere to be found, selfless people with such firm faith that they care not at all about their own safety but only about honoring God?

Where are the "Ruths" we need now, people who are selflessly, lovingly devoted to God while nearly everyone in our society seems to be selfishly in love with themselves?

Where do we find today's "Davids," people who don't care one bit about the enormity of their opponent because they have great faith in their big, undefeatable God and are happy to risk personal harm to see his name exalted?

Where can we find a few "Nehemiahs," those who recognize that there will always be fierce opposition to God's agenda but who will do whatever is necessary to ensure God's plan prevails, no matter what?

Where do we go to find our "Esthers," people passionate about preserving and passing on an eternally significant legacy to the next generation, so they don't forget their God and learn the hard way that obedience to him brings blessing, while disobedience brings discipline?

Can we find an army of "Shadrachs," "Meshachs," and "Abednegos," threatened men, women, boys, and girls who refuse to forsake their God and are willing to stand for him—at the risk of their own well-being—when all that would be needed to secure lives of comfort and convenience would be a little cowardly compromise?

And where are our contemporary apostles, those who recognize we've reached a "we must obey God rather than man" moment in our nation and in many places around the world, people who defy the threats of mere mortals because they love and respect their God, and care about the proclamation of truth?

If you see the Bible primarily as a book of exceptions rather than examples, you'll never rise to the level of humble, courageous living that is necessary to change lives, culture, and nations. It's time we stop missing the point by focusing on our being unlikely, incapable, ordinary people—because unlikely, incapable, ordinary people are the only kinds of people God has ever had to use. We are the only lumps of clay in God's pottery barn.

If you see the Bible primarily as a book of exceptions rather than examples, you'll never rise to the level of humble, courageous living that is necessary to change lives, culture, and nations.

The truth is that you have much more in common with the people in the Bible whom God used mightily to shape history and civilizations than you realize. Apart from Jesus Christ, God has only and always had nothing but imperfect, fallen, recovering hypocrites and sinners with whom to work. Recognizing this reality will set you free and help you stand up and speak out while others are telling you to sit down and shut up.

It's time for you and me—and throngs of ordinary people just like you and me—to arise and become the willing army of courageous, humble heroes and underdogs we desperately need at this very time of testing. To be specific, God wants to use, and can use, *you*. It's time you and I become *willing* to do what others won't—what we haven't been willing to do with resolute determination, until, perhaps, now. It's time for tenacious, humble courage to arise on a massive scale, throughout the nation—not in some distant time in the future, when it will be too late, but *now.*

IN A NUTSHELL

COURAGEOUS HUMILITY IN ACTION

Practical Things You Can Ponder and Practice Right Now

- Do you think the Bible is primarily a book of exceptions or examples? Your answer to this single question will determine the rest of your life. How has your answer up to this moment in your life been impacting how you live?
- Is Moses' plea your plea? Are you hungry for the presence of God in your life—and in the lives of others you encounter—above all else? Have you settled for success without God?
- If the apathy and cowardice so prevalent today were the norm during World War II, we'd all be speaking German, Japanese, or Italian—with the consequences affecting far

more than our language. Have you allowed yourself to become apathetic to what's happening in society? Have you given up on people, and in the process, even given up on God? What would society be like if everyone had your approach to God and life?

- If you limit what you *will* do for God, you limit what you *can* do for God. Have you in any way limited what you will do for God? How might that be limiting your ability to stand up with courageous humility against the evils we see rising all around?
- We are the only lumps of clay in God's pottery barn. Apart from Jesus Christ, God has only and always had nothing but hypocrites and sinners with whom to work. Have you made the mistake of thinking your past, and even your present tendencies, are obstacles for God? Why not get into the habit of acknowledging your hypocrisy and sin the moment they come to your attention and ask God to overcome them all?

4

Intolerance, the New Tolerance

"Woe to those who call evil good
and good evil,
who put darkness for light
and light for darkness,
who put bitter for sweet
and sweet for bitter."

—ISAIAH 5:20

A very kind, wealthy man in a well-known city was nearing the end of his life. As he reflected on his legacy, he wanted to make a final, positive contribution to the city and people he loved so much by leaving something behind they could all enjoy long after he was gone. He decided to fund the construction of the city's tallest, most beautiful building.

Two architectural firms were invited to bid for the honor of bringing his vision into reality. The first firm's estimate was three times as high, with the work taking four times as long as the second firm to complete. Curious about the vast differences, the wealthy man brought in the chief architect of each firm, one at a time, to discuss their concepts and approaches to construction.

The differences in time and cost came down to two totally different philosophies. The first architect was bent on building the tallest building in the city. The second described his unorthodox approach as follows:

> "The fastest, most cost-effective way to get you the tallest building in this city is to choose the building you like most and then have me arrange to tear down everything else, clear out to the city limits. Whatever is left standing will be the tallest building. I'm pretty sure it will also be the most beautiful too!" he exclaimed, with an accompanying laugh that shook the room.

Which architect do you think the wealthy, kind philanthropist chose to create the capstone for his life's legacy? I have a hunch that your guess is right on the money.

There are two ways to guarantee the tallest building in a city. The first way is simply to build the tallest building. The second is to tear down all the surrounding structures. Whatever is left standing will clearly be the tallest building.[1]

I wish I were merely talking about a building and architects, but I'm not. I'm talking about the ways increasing numbers of people interact with one another in this twenty-first century. People (unfortunately, many Christians included) have become experts at tearing others down as they strive to build themselves up. Many debates begin with the issues and quickly escalate into personal attacks that only make matters worse. America today resembles a group of contemptuous middle-school children who never learned the principles of healthy communication and conflict resolution. I imagine that if it were possible, our conduct would be enough to make even God himself sick.

What I call "reverse intolerance" is all the rage these days. Most literally. It has become a pandemic, with a growing number of people presenting themselves as tolerant, loving, calm, compassionate, fair-minded, and reasonable—but their actions betray them. Express even remote concern for the protection of the American border, and you are marginalized as a "xenophobe."[2] Embrace the historic, biblical view of heterosexual marriage, and you are instantly called a "homophobe." Raise questions about the transgender issue, or embrace the view that there are only two genders presented in the Bible, male and female, and you are labeled a "bigot" opposing someone else's civil rights. The ensuing attack, however, will resemble nothing civil at all. These examples are but the tip of the reverse intolerance iceberg.

Historic Christianity, the religion of love, is in the crosshairs. Anyone who embraces traditional Judeo-Christian values is public enemy number one. The opposition comes courtesy of the love haters. They seem to be in love with hate. They don't want a bigger table around which Americans can share a meal called *diversity*. They want to remove the chairs of anyone who disagrees with them—and lock them out of the room. What they really want is *exclusivity*. In fact, they demand it.

Hate has become the new love, and love has become the new hate. Wrong is right, and right is wrong.

A new breed of bigot—hypocritically obstinate, overflowing with boisterous prejudice—is masquerading as open-minded, caring, and compassionate. Hate has become the new love, and love has become the new hate. Wrong is right, and right is wrong. The reverse-intolerant are out and about, in full force, and we are just beginning to feel the weight of their power. They speak of fairness and insist upon it—until you disagree with them. Then they go into attack mode.

Suicide Bombers, #Haters, and the New #DoubleStandard

The reverse-intolerant will not rest until they control the media, politics, theology, and even the education of young children. Yes, they want your children—and everyone's children—because they know that if they can educate people at a young age, their worldview will become the way of the land. Is it fearmongering to say so? Not at all. It's a matter of fact, and we must begin to face it head-on. If you think there is not a concerted effort to gain access to children so they can be indoctrinated with neoorthodox morality opposed to historic, Judeo-Christian teaching, it's time to get your head out of your bucket.

In fairness, many Christians have acted, and are acting, in some of the same ways as the love haters, which is a great irony. Many of us have not been very loving in the ways we have communicated our disagreements. We've wanted people to tolerate our views while reviling not just their views but also the people behind them. Our values may be right, but our methods have, at times, been wrong, even, at times, sinful. It's time we make it right. Let the love haters play underhandedly. Real Christ-followers must rise above it all, and when we do we will see God honored powerfully—and relationships mended.

Christians and love haters may be able to find common ground on some issues, and even some legislation. We may even be able to peacefully coexist. I realize that some Christians may take issue with this suggestion, thinking I am compromising on biblical truth—but thinking so would be a mistake. What I'm suggesting is that we hold the line on our doctrine, but hold our tongues in our diatribes. In many instances, it's the *manner* in which we present our views that lacks manners and hampers our persuasion. For this, a great many of us need to repent and change our approach.

Consider Jesus; he was no pushover. He took an uncompromising stance against sin while being a champion of love. We who say we are following him should be known for the same. In many cases our focus has been to pummel our opponents, whatever the cost. Often our approach has cost us our witness and converts. Mature Christians must debate in ways that lead people to the feet of Christ, where there, they find the acceptance, peace, and forgiveness that can only be found at his table.

Paul's advice is practical for us today: "Let your conversation be always full of grace, seasoned with salt, so that you may know how to answer everyone" (Col. 4:6).

For Christians, it must never be just about winning arguments. It must be about winning souls. Therein lies the fundamental way in which we transform culture. Minds may be shaped by strong argument, but hearts are only pierced through mercy, compassion, and that thing for which we Christians are supposed to be known, that many of us seem to have forgotten. Care to take a stab at what it is? It's a four-letter word—and it's a beauty. It's the thing by which all people on earth will recognize a real Christ-follower, and it's time we rediscover it in the midst of the culture war in which we find ourselves immersed. The word is *l-o-v-e*.

Lawrence and the Nighttime Bible Reading Society

Lawrence is the quintessential love hater.[3] He has mastered the art of reverse intolerance nearly as well as Leonardo da Vinci handled paper and ink. At one time he, too, was a pastor, and we shared many things in common. But everything changed dramatically after Lawrence quit his long-standing, full-time job as a pastor to work at another church. That's where he was fired—and he became the anti-Lawrence. The destructive root of bitterness took up residence in his heart.

He got another job as a pastor at yet another church. It started as a *part-time* position serving *only* on Sundays, but the job did what I think he wanted it to do: establish his credibility and gain him an audience. Today Lawrence has made a sadly successful career from his bitterness, playing upon the disenfranchisement and bitterness of others. He spends his days blogging, speaking, and complaining, especially about evangelical, conservative Christians—people who embrace historic Judeo-Christian values. His target became the very group of people from which he came.[4]

Lawrence's approach models, down to the letter, the exact things against which he rails—intolerance, bias, and bigotry. Each time one of his op-eds is published, or he self-publishes one of his #double-standard blogs, or he posts something on social media, Lawrence blows himself up. He has become a social media suicide bomber, ready to detonate any time he gets within range of someone who does not share his views, especially evangelical Christians.

Lawrence's bitterness and hatred have deceived him into thinking the people he meets at speaking engagements are real friends, and that online, virtual communities are a healthy substitute for real, face-to-face friendships and fellowship. He has not yet realized that the majority of his new "friendships" are actually conditioned upon a common hatred toward their mutual enemies. Hate has a way of making strange bedfellows.

Like a rafter caught in a whirlpool, Lawrence needs someone to rescue him from the torrent of his intolerance. He needs the Jesus of the Bible—not the Jesus of select portions of the Bible that the love haters like to emphasize at the exclusion of others, but the real Jesus who authored *all* of it.

Lawrence is an unintentional card-carrying member of what I call the "Nighttime Bible Reading Society." He might as well read the Bible at night, lights off, sunglasses on, with one eye closed. Such a pursuit would make it impossible to get a clear understanding of the real Jesus and the heart and mind of God. Cherry-picking certain verses of the Bible over others to suit our fancy always results in recreating God in our own image. It's foolish and outright dangerous.

I hope you are concerned about Lawrence and the people he now misleads. The love haters are confused and deceived, and they are rapidly multiplying. We truly need to pray for them and the people who swallow their bait. I hope every one of us who says we're following Christ prays for our enemies—and even those enemies, who, blinded by bitterness, mistake us as theirs. Deep down, it's my hope that Lawrence is just going through a phase and that he will one day humble himself and return to the lover of his soul with a fervor fit to make the prodigal son jealous (Luke 15:11–31).[5]

Until such time, Lawrence, and people like him, cannot be ignored, because their roots of anger and bitterness are infecting the nation and world. Hate is a powerful agent of change, and it is transforming our nation even as you read this. Lawrence teaches us that failure to resolve deep-seated wounds results not only in self-destructive behavior but also inflicts deep, unnecessary pain on others.[6]

Legion

Lawrence is not alone. He is legion, and he is growing. This legion will use intimidation, legislation, journalism, the education system, social media, and the redefinition of basic words to force all who disagree with it to sit down and shut up once and for all. This is why you and I must stand up and speak out—with diplomacy and grace, with fearless, unapologetic courage. If we don't, those who call evil good and good evil, who mistake darkness for light and light for darkness, and bitter for sweet and sweet for bitter, will win—and they will do it all in the names of "love" and "tolerance," with smiles on their faces and deep-seated hatred, bitterness, and intolerance in their hearts.

This legion now threatens to soon outnumber us all. It is certainly out-shouting us, making sure the world hears and fears it. If it succeeds, it will be a dark day for America—and all of civilization. Isaiah 5:20 provides a stark warning to those bent on perverting the truth:

> *Woe to those who call evil good*
> *and good evil,*
> *who put darkness for light*
> *and light for darkness,*
> *who put bitter for sweet*
> *and sweet for bitter!* (ESV)

It's been said that "all that is necessary for the triumph of evil is for good people to do nothing."[7] At no other time in history has there been a greater need for courageous humility. Unless we learn how to be simultaneously humble and courageous, reverse intolerance and hatred will become the norm in America. Intolerance will, once and for all, be the new tolerance.

The humility and courage needed to handle reverse intolerance are not traits with which we are born. Be encouraged because they are learned and developed. A more-than-adequate teacher of these traits is found in Jesus, the perfect embodiment of humble courage. Now is a great time to turn our eyes upon Jesus. He was the master at standing up and speaking out. If we stop confusing mere Bible knowledge for its application—if we follow Jesus closely—his heart and method will begin to rub off on us, and everyone we encounter will begin to see him at this very hour when we need to see him most.

IN A NUTSHELL

COURAGEOUS HUMILITY IN ACTION

Practical Things You Can Ponder and Practice Right Now

- Stand up and speak out, but don't knock others down in the process.
- Courageous humility is not something we are born with. It's something we learn and develop—if we are intentional.
- A legion of love haters is on the rise—people masquerading as calm, tolerant, inclusive, compassionate, and reasonable—but it is nothing of the sort. Do you care about its opinions more than the opinions of God? What might happen to our children, and to our society, if we allow the legion of love haters to intimidate and silence us?
- Colossians 4:6 says, "Let your conversation be always full of grace, seasoned with salt, so that you may know how to answer everyone." Does this approach characterize your conversations, even when there is strong disagreement?
- Does the way you debate lead people to the feet of Jesus or result in them being trampled under your feet? Minds may be shaped by strong argument, but hearts are only

pierced through mercy, compassion, and that thing we Christians are supposed to be known for, that many of us seem to have forgotten: l-o-v-e. Remember, it's not about merely winning arguments, but about winning souls. This is how culture is truly transformed.

- The best way to learn how to develop humble courage is to study and follow the life and teachings of Jesus Christ and those in history who followed him closely and left positive legacies. The moment you learn something new about Jesus, immediately put it into practice as *your* new way of life. When we put off humility and courage, we are embracing arrogance and fear by default.

5

Resurrecting and Defending Religious Freedom

Congress shall make no law respecting
an establishment of religion, or
prohibiting the free exercise thereof; or
abridging the freedom of speech . . .

—THE FIRST AMENDMENT TO THE UNITED STATES CONSTITUTION

America's battle over religious freedom is like a twisting, turning, often frightening roller-coaster ride. And while there are pauses along the way, there is no sign that this ride will come to an end. The uncertain twists and turns of the religious freedom roller coaster are sure to make any person of faith—and anyone who really understands the First Amendment—uneasy. We must learn to stomach the ride so that we don't grow weary and give up where and when our perseverance is needed most. Our children, and the kind of nation we will be, depend upon our dogged refusal to sit down and shut up about the most important God-given freedom we have: the freedom to love and enjoy our Creator, and to help others do the same.

Many people of faith are doing little more than acknowledging that the free exercise of religion in America (and globally) is under aggressive attack. Unwittingly leaning too heavily on the Rapture and the second coming of Christ as escape clauses God never meant them to be, many Christians assume we won't be here when things get really bad, so why bother. As a result, many of us are not living as "salt shakers," working diligently to spread truth and love every chance we get. This amounts to the serious sin of apathy with enslavement as the result.

Religious persecution is about forcing people of faith to sit down and shut up, to keep their God in a box. But courageous humility is about letting him out of the box we've allowed him to be shoved into. It's about standing up and speaking out while there is still freedom—and time—to do so. I don't want to merely educate you about the rapidly growing trend of hostilities toward religious freedom, but to help you respond constructively, with courageous humility—for the sake of freedom itself, the welfare of future generations, and the sheer glory of God.

God in a Box[1]

The First Amendment is the leading domino of American law. Without it, there is no America as originally envisioned. Our Founding Fathers recognized the "unalienable rights" given to us by our Creator: life, liberty, and the pursuit of happiness. We cannot enjoy these rights, however, if we are hindered in the area of religious expression.

Our unalienable rights aren't given to us by people or even by the Constitution; they are given to us by God. To attack them is to attack far more than just freedom. It is to attack freedom's Creator. It is, in a very real sense, the ultimate form of bullying because it is to bully God. Freedom, and the republic of America, rises or falls on whether or not the First Amendment is protected or undermined.

The First Amendment includes two religious clauses: the establishment clause and the free exercise clause. The establishment clause is the phrase "Congress shall make no law respecting an establishment of religion." What's getting lost these days is the phrase immediately following it, the free exercise clause: "or prohibiting the free exercise thereof." In other words, the First Amendment does not merely prohibit the establishment of a religion by the government, it also protects the ability to exercise one's religion without infringement by the government. Yet it is the free exercise of religion that is especially, and increasingly, under attack in the United States and around the world.

Our unalienable rights aren't given to us by people; . . . *they are given to us by God.* To attack them is to attack far more than just freedom. It is to attack freedom's Creator. . . . It is to bully God.

You should probably care about the two religious clauses in the First Amendment a lot more than you have up to this point. Your concern should lead you to take constructive, courageous action to stand up and speak out any and every time you see the free exercise of religion endangered. If Congress is strictly forbidden from making any law that will prohibit the free exercise of religion, as the First Amendment clearly says, then we should embrace it, thank our God, and fight vehemently for the protection of religious freedom every single time it is threatened.

Where Religious Freedom Is Under Attack—and How We Can (and Must) Fight Back

In broad terms, religious freedom is under attack in four areas: the public square, schools specifically, houses of worship and religious institutions, and the military. What follows is merely a sampling of a growing list of intolerant, discriminatory acts against Americans who take their faith seriously, whose God-given rights are being increasingly targeted in the name of tolerance and equality. As you read, consider how you, your family, and your friends can stand up and speak out with humble, courageous action to ensure that the First Amendment to our Constitution is protected. Its demise would be catastrophic for people of all faiths.

Attacks Against Religious Freedom in the Public Square

The Case of the Good Doctor

Dr. Eric Walsh was hired in 2014 by the State of Georgia to work in the Department of Public Health as a senior official. The State of Georgia, however, fired him after examining sermons Dr. Walsh preached (as a lay leader) at his church. Dr. Walsh filed a discrimination lawsuit against the state, in accordance with the US Equal Employment Opportunity Commission (EEOC), saying it was unlawful to fire him "solely on his religious beliefs."[2]

On September 28, 2016, the State of Georgia tried to compel Dr. Walsh to hand over all his sermons and sermon notes—including transcripts. An aggressive counteroffensive launched by First Liberty Institute resulted in the State of Georgia withdrawing its request, and on February 7, 2017, the state paid $225,000 to settle Dr. Walsh's lawsuit.[3]

This case is a perfect example of how important it is to stand up, speak out, and fight back when facing religious persecution. Such battles are not at all exercises in futility but are expressions of real faith being flexed with humility and courage when the pressure is on. These are the kinds of battles people of faith must fight if we hope to protect our religious freedom.

Attempts to Prohibit Public Prayer

Starting in 1999, the town of Greece, New York, began the practice of opening its board meetings with prayer—until they were sued. The district court upheld that the prayers were permissible, but the Second Circuit reversed their decision, holding that the prayers "'impermissibly affiliated the town with a single creed, Christianity,' because most of the prayers before the town board—along with most of the churches in the town—were Christian."[4] The US Supreme Court reversed the Second Circuit decision, however, and ruled that the prayers "are constitutional and that the government cannot interfere in the content of the prayers or require an artificial diversity of religions. The Supreme Court made clear that the government cannot require 'non-sectarian' prayers but must allow each person who prays to pray according to that person's conscience."[5]

The Court held that the prayers given by the clergy at the town board meetings comport with a long tradition, going back to the first Congress, of opening legislatures with prayer. The Court said, "Adults often encounter speech they find disagreeable; and an Establishment Clause violation is not made out any time a person experiences a sense of affront from the expression of contrary religious views in a legislative forum, especially where, as here, any member of the public is welcome in turn to offer an invocation reflecting his or her own convictions."[6]

The Separation of Church and State Myth

The phrase "separation of church and state" is not found anywhere in the Declaration of Independence or the Constitution, nor was that phrase ever intended to portray a prohibition of religious freedom in America. Instead, the phrase "separation of church and state" comes from a letter that Thomas Jefferson wrote to the Danbury Baptist Association in 1802 to reiterate Jefferson's commitment to religious freedom for the Baptists.[7] The Supreme Court's own words affirm that America's history and traditions recognize the role religion plays in our nation, including in our government. People of faith need to rise and shine with heads held high, understanding that history proves that the "separation of church and state" mantra is a historically weak one used by liberal, revisionist historians bent on marginalizing people of faith.

The next time someone pulls out the "separation of church and state" myth, remember *Town of Greece, New York, v. Galloway*, and the very words of the Supreme Court. Your liberal, revisionist-historian friends will cringe, being utterly incapable of any substantive rebuttal if you humbly, diplomatically quote the Court's words, provided above, verbatim. The Court's words settle the matter.[8]

Diversity or Discrimination?

In the name of diversity training, the United States Social Security Administration instituted a policy requiring all employees to watch a seventeen-minute video that promotes LGBTQ (lesbian, gay, bisexual, transgender, and questioning) lifestyles. A Christian employee, David Hall, with a career spanning fourteen years with the agency, diplomatically refused, and was reprimanded and suspended without pay.[9] Mr. Hall could even end up losing his job because of his refusal to watch the video.

No doubt, *militant** LGBTQ activists will argue that Mr. Hall was free to work elsewhere—no one forced him to stay in his job. True, but let's apply that logic consistently. Would those within the militant LGBTQ community likewise insist that gay couples soliciting wedding cakes from non-obliging Christian bakers simply find different bakers who would oblige? Most likely they would not. The case that follows is even more alarming, illustrating the double standard that is often applied by the militant LGBTQ community when they encounter people who will not applaud their lifestyle.[10]

Forced Reprogramming—in America

You may have heard the story of Aaron and Melissa Klein, owners of the Sweetcakes by Melissa bakery in Oregon, who were driven out of business after they refused to bake a cake for a same-sex wedding.[11] But you may not be nearly as familiar with the alarming case of Jack Phillips, a devout Christian and owner of the Masterpiece Cakeshop, Inc., who was approached by a gay couple to make their wedding cake. He refused because he felt doing so would be akin to celebrating a practice he believes God does not endorse and was found guilty of violating Colorado's Anti-Discrimination Act (CADA).[12] As a result, he was ordered to stop conducting any further business by a Colorado court. But that is not all.

As part of the court order, Phillips and his employees were compelled to undergo sensitivity training (including his eighty-seven-year-old mother) to force them to comply with a state law designed to prevent discrimination against same-sex couples. He was also ordered to provide reports to the state (for two years, on a quarterly basis) should he ever choose to deny baking services or

---

* It is important to distinguish between those who struggle with their sexual identity or even celebrate a LGBTQ lifestyle and who seek a peaceful, noninvasive means of doing so from those who *demand* that their lifestyles be celebrated by *everyone*.

products to anyone, for any reason. The Colorado Supreme Court upheld the lower court's decision, denying Phillips's appeal.[13] The US Supreme Court has agreed to hear the case on December 5, 2017. (At the time of publication, the ruling had not yet been made.)[14]

The American Civil Liberties Union (ACLU) issued a statement about the case, saying, "Religious freedom is undoubtedly an important American value, but so is the right to be treated equally under the law, free from discrimination."[15]

In truth, religious freedom is not merely "an important American value," as the ACLU stated. It is freedom given to us by God, not the government. Such freedom is the bedrock of our entire way of life here in America. If we do not have the freedom of religious expression, as protected by the First Amendment, then life, liberty, and the pursuit of happiness are important only as concepts, not as realities. The exercise of one's faith is central to the experience of true liberty and the pursuit of happiness. And life, for people of genuine faith, is found largely through the expression of faith. For the faithful, there is no such thing as life without the freedom to worship and serve the Creator.

So What?

What the courts have done in these instances strikes at the very core of religious freedom in America and undermines how love for God may be manifest—or even outright prohibited—through the insistence of tolerance, in the name of preventing discrimination and promoting civil rights. Tolerance is replacing freedom as the supreme American value, but this replacement must be resisted, not celebrated. Tolerance at the expense of freedom is not tolerance at all. It's politically correct language for the exact opposite: *intolerance.*

In none of the instances mentioned above are any people of faith harassing or hindering members of another race, religion, or sex. They are not attacking their beliefs, lifestyles, or livelihoods. *This is crucial to understand.* Yet in every instance above, we see people of faith being aggressively targeted and attacked, with attempts being made to compel them to compromise their religious convictions and not merely accept, but also *celebrate*, alternatives. This is to force someone to choose between God and government. It is those who are seeking to silence people of faith who are behaving radically out of step with the Constitution and the idea of protecting the free exercise of one's faith.

The words of Jesus should be especially clear and dear to Christians and important for any court of law to consider, because these are not just the opinions of people we are debating. Jesus said, "If you *love* me, *keep my commands. . . . Anyone who loves me will obey my teaching*" (John 14:15, 23, emphasis added).

Tolerance at the expense of freedom is not tolerance at all. It's politically correct language for the exact opposite: *intolerance*.

This is not about cakes being baked. It's about faith getting fried. We should fight—humbly and relentlessly—for religious freedom. The attempt to couch the continuously morphing sexual revolution as a civil rights issue, to protect people from "discrimination," is resulting in the passage of laws that *force* people to violate their God-given, unalienable right to worship and honor their Creator as the first, most noble, and all-encompassing calling in life. This is not something to passively resist. It's something we must resist with courageous humility.

If we were to apply the same logic of the militant[16] LGBTQ community consistently, a case could be made for doctors in America to be compelled to provide abortions, under the principle that noncompliance is a violation of the civil rights of a mother-to-be. By the same reasoning, we will speed toward the day when even private schools and homeschoolers will be required to teach LGBTQ values—or any such teaching that the state or federal governments may deem necessary—as a matter of promoting tolerance, equality, and civil rights. Imagine five-, six-, and seven-year-old children being so indoctrinated.

What are people of faith to do? Stand up. Speak out. Be faithful to God, regardless of human opinion. Leonard Ravenhill said it this way: "God's opinion of man is fixed. Man's opinion of God is fluid. Trust and obey or rust and decay."[17] Remember that obedience to God is more important than any other pursuit in all of life. In this new era of reverse intolerance, where fear of people threatens to turn many—perhaps even you—away from God, it is vital to passionately embrace Jesus' words:

> What good is it for someone to gain the whole world, yet forfeit their soul? Or what can anyone give in exchange for their soul? If anyone is ashamed of me and my words in this adulterous and sinful generation, the Son of Man will be ashamed of them when he comes in his Father's glory with the holy angels. (Mark 8:36–38)

Attacks Against Religious Freedom in Schools

Kneeling Warrior Booted

In Bremerton, Washington, high school coach Joe Kennedy was fired for praying on a football field—after the game was over and the players had already left the field.[18] His practice of praying at the fifty-yard line after games began seven years earlier, but in 2015, he was fired for offering a prayer after a football game. In an effort to regain his job, Coach Kennedy filed a lawsuit in 2016 against the Bremerton School District.[19]

Was Coach Kennedy's expression of faith infringing on anyone else's behavior? Was he compelling anyone else to celebrate his behavior? The answer to both questions is most certainly not. How then is it legal to prohibit Coach Kennedy's religious expression? The US Court of Appeals for the Ninth Circuit heard oral arguments on June 12, 2017. In August, the Court ruled in favor of the school district, that coach Kennedy had no right to publicly pray on school grounds if done "in the presence of students and spectators."

Think about what this means for people of *all* faiths—that a school can require a teacher to sit down and shut up about the most precious aspect of his or her life: the freedom to openly love and enjoy his or her God, even if no one else is being hindered or coerced by his or her conduct. Are you okay with that?

The Court's decision is a prime example of reverse intolerance against people of faith, and it contradicts our God-given First Amendment–protected right of freedom of religious expression.

Source Censorship?

This case hits me close to home because Phillipsburg, New Jersey, is the neighboring town to where I grew up. It's also where my mother lived just prior to her passing.

The Phillipsburg School District fired a substitute teacher, Walt Tutka, because he handed a Bible to a student.[20] Interestingly, the student asked for the Bible after Mr. Tutka had referenced the Bible verse, "The last will be first and the first will be last" (Matt. 20:16). After the student made consistent requests to be told the origin of the phrase, the teacher obliged, finding the quote in the Bible and showing it to the student. The school fired Mr. Tutka when it learned that the teacher offered the Bible to the student after learning the student did not have one.[21]

In an encouraging turn-around, on December 15, 2014, the EEOC issued a determination letter supporting Tutka, and he was reinstated as a substitute teacher on May 11, 2017. The case demonstrates the importance of persistence in the battle against religious discrimination. Standing up and speaking out takes time, energy, and patience, but it is also incredibly rewarding and beneficial to everyone.

Attacks Against Religious Freedom Toward Churches and Houses of Worship

Opulent Death?

Wanting to move into a larger facility, Opulent Life Church in Holly Springs, Mississippi, began a search for new property.[22] However, the City of Holly Springs stipulated a requirement that applied only to churches—that the church obtain the approval of 60 percent of all nearby property owners in order to proceed with the land acquisition. The church sued the city for violation of the US Constitution, the Institutionalized Persons Act, and the Religious Land Use.[23]

The district court issued a temporary restraining order and an injunction on October 18, 2012, forcing the City of Holly Springs to stop enforcing its revised zoning ordinance. A settlement agreement with the city was reached that allowed Opulent Life Church to relocate to the downtown area of Holly Springs and for the city to pay $100,000 in damages, costs, and attorneys' fees. If the people of Opulent Life Church had confused apathy or fatalism with sovereignty of God, and given up their fight, the outcome could have been totally different. Once again, humble resistance proved fruitful, not futile.

A Texas Sabbath

Toras Chaim, a small Jewish congregation in North Dallas, met in a neighborhood home because members of the congregation do not drive on the Sabbath. A neighbor filed a lawsuit against the congregation to stop their use of the home for worship, saying that their use of a home in that particular neighborhood was a violation of the homeowner's association (HOA) covenants and restrictions.[24] Toras Chaim was successful in defeating the HOA efforts to shut them down. A new attempt, however, is underway by the City of Dallas to sue Toras Chaim because they do not have a religious certificate of occupancy. The matter is still pending a final outcome at the time of this writing.[25]

Attacks Against Religious Freedom in the Military

Can't a Chaplain Counsel?

Wes Modder, a decorated Navy SEAL and chaplain who served our nation for nineteen commendable years, faced dismissal "because he provided pastoral counseling consistent with his religious beliefs about sexual conduct outside of marriage."[26] He is a Christian, affiliated with the Assemblies of God, and was following what his faith and Bible consistently teach about sexual morality. Although it was a close call, Chaplain Modder was cleared of all wrongdoing. In 2016, he retired from the navy and was awarded the Meritorious Service Medal. He now serves as the lead pastor at Stone Church in Orland Park, Illinois.

Imagine if Chaplain Modder hadn't fought back. A dangerous precedent would have been set, emboldening those who think people of faith can be told to sit down and shut up, when what they really need to do is stand up and speak out.

Same-Sex Sizzle

Phillip Monk was a senior master sergeant (not a chaplain) with a nineteen-year admirable service record in the United States Air

Force.[27] He returned from deployment to find himself assigned to a new commander—a practicing lesbian who asked him for his opinion about same-sex marriage. Monk initially refused to answer, stating that his views on the issue were irrelevant to his job. The commander, however, demanded that he share his views, and Monk confirmed his view of biblical marriage being the union of one man and one woman. The commander relieved Monk of his duties and reassigned him—an apparent act of retaliation for Monk's biblical views.

Initially, air force investigators charged Monk with making false statements, but the charges were dismissed on October 1, 2013. He was awarded the Meritorious Service Medal in February 2014. He retired honorably in January 2015.[28]

The retribution Monk faced at the hands of his lesbian commander is very similar to that experienced by bakers Aaron and Melissa Klein and Jack Phillips. He was not seeking to force his religious views on anyone else. He simply wanted to honor his God and live his faith and was persecuted for his attempts. His humble courage paid off, and we, too, can follow his honorable example.

The "We Can't Legislate Morality" Myth

The idea that we can't legislate morality is a myth. *In reality, we do it all the time.* All legislation is an attempt to impose someone's morality on the masses. It is merely a matter of whose morality is imposed. There is no getting around it. If laws of any kind are to be passed, they will be based on standards of what people embrace as right or wrong. It's impossible to pass laws otherwise.

If we allow ourselves to be apathetic, lazy, and detached, if we cry *uncle* now and sit down and shut up, we will guarantee and accelerate the time when houses of worship will be fined and even forced to close their doors (remember the bakeries) for teaching historic, biblical truth. We must not mistake fatalism for faith. We must stand up, speak out, and never give up, so that we ensure pastors, rabbis, and other religious leaders will not face fines or imprisonment for simply feeding truth to their flocks.

Board members of religious institutions should pay especially close attention to the attacks on religious freedom, because boards and the institutions they govern will not escape if we fail to rise up and stand strong. If we sit by and allow what's been happening to continue, without resistance, thinking the battle is too far removed for us to be concerned, we will invite defeat. Even if we fight hard and lose a battle here and there, we know that doing what is right and honorable to God is always in fashion, regardless of the outcome this side of eternity. Our lot will be far less troubling if we will let humble courage arise and spread throughout the nation.

Legislators, Judges, and Laws Matter

The attacks endured by the people I've mentioned in this chapter could be experienced by just about anyone who takes his or her faith seriously and is challenged by someone who forces the issue. Each case demonstrates the dangerous reality that the First Amendment is under direct assault, in the name of tolerance and civil rights, in the name of preventing discrimination. All along, however, a new brand of discrimination and reverse intolerance has arisen, and is being celebrated.

Each of the cases in this chapter illustrates the importance of electing legislators who will uphold, protect, and defend the Constitution of the United States. They all demonstrate how important it is to have judges who understand and defend our First Amendment rights. We must quickly come to understand that if only those who reject historic, Judeo-Christian values—and who possess a newfangled interpretation of our First Amendment rights—are elected to office, freedom in America will come to mean something very different from what it has meant throughout our history.

If those of us who embrace historic, Judeo-Christian values and love our Constitution fail to participate in the political process and do not uphold, protect, and defend the Constitution of the United States by doing so, we will guarantee the destruction of our religious freedom—not only for ourselves, but for people of every faith. We might as well be the ones toppling the first domino, starting the chain reaction that sends America's freedoms of speech and religion to crash down onto the table. Sadly, this could happen while the First Amendment remains only on paper, becoming nothing more than a relic of the past, a historic document that no longer has any practical application as the law of the land it was penned to be.

Christian Call Out

To be fair, many within the conservative Christian community have practiced what I think is a huge double standard toward the LGBTQ community. In many cases we've settled for winning battles and lost sight of winning the war. The war is not against people, but against ideologies and sin. The war is about learning to speak truth with love so that people are drawn toward Jesus, not driven from him. In many ways a lot of Christians still seem inept at doing this. I think it's time for many to rediscover the way the Bible tells us we are to love people and how we are to proclaim and live the truth.

Many people who endorse heterosexual marriage have been guilty of strong-arming and bullying opponents—the very same tactics that the militant LGBTQ community has mastered against people who embrace the historic, Judeo-Christian view of heterosexual marriage. Neither their tactics nor those of conservative people of faith are justifiable. And the wrongs committed by some conservatives do not add up to a free pass for the militant LGBTQ community to strong-arm the heterosexual world into embracing their lifestyles. (Bullying—by anyone—is always wrong and should always be confronted. If a Christian is guilty of bullying, loving a position more than a person, a significant bit of repentance is in order.)

As a conservative Christian, the pastor of a large church, and the leader of a somewhat global ministry, I think I'm in a position to lovingly, patiently call my conservative friends out—with a genuine amount of fear and trembling. If we're honest with one another, honest with many who struggle with their sexual identity and attractions, and honest with God, we have to admit that many among our ranks have been far less than Christlike in their actions. We within the "religion of love" have often demonstrated a great deal of hate. We have recited our tagline "hate the sin, love the sinner," but too often we have hated both. This nonsense needs to stop, as it has resulted in many leaving the established church, feeling rejected by a God who wants nothing more than to deeply embrace them.

Wrongly, many Christians view and treat people who engage in same-sex sexual activity as if they were committing an unpardonable sin.[29] Meanwhile, pride, disunity, gossip, slander, pornography, and family neglect—along with endeavors to keep these sins hidden as we maintain our church faces—run rampant in the lives of many who insist they are Christ-followers.

Christians need to apply the Bible consistently, not selectively. The thinking and behavior among us is nothing less than textbook hypocrisy, an exercise in absurdity. Many conservative Christians need to genuinely repent, with tears of remorse leading to deep changes in word and deed. We need to live the kinds of lives that make people jealous, in good ways, of our joy, peace, love, and values. Is your life worthy of that kind of jealousy? If you are really following Christ, it will be.

In the next chapter, I want to share how we who embrace historic, Judeo-Christian views of sex and sexuality can humbly speak the truth in love with great impact—without even a hint of bigotry, homophobia, or hatred. Our words and deeds will have much greater effect if we first win the right to stand up and speak out by developing a proven track record marked by genuine love for people.

IN A NUTSHELL

COURAGEOUS HUMILITY IN ACTION

Practical Things You Can Ponder and Practice Right Now

- Have you confused fatalism with faith? Have you used God's sovereignty as an excuse for your own apathy?
- Are you guilty of the "Jesus said things would get worse anyway" argument, using it as an excuse for not doing what is right, regardless of the outcome here and now? People with real faith do what is right as a matter of honoring God, regardless of the outcome this side of eternity.
- All legislation is an attempt to impose someone's morality on the majority—it's simply a matter of whose morality should be imposed. Do you have a right to complain about legislators, judges, and laws if you sit on the sidelines while they are being elected, appointed, and enacted? Your children and your children's children have every right to one day ask you what you did while Judeo-Christian values were being undermined. Are you doing all you can, right now, to fight with humble courage for their religious freedom?
- What would happen to Judeo-Christian values in

America if everyone followed your lead? Would biblical values be upheld and promoted or struck down and belittled?

- Based on how you are now fighting for religious freedom, what might your children think about your concern for them, and for God, years from now?
- Are you guilty of strong-arming and bullying people who don't share your views about sexuality, or do you express yourself with a clear love and compassion for those who disagree, and toward those who may be confused or struggling with their sexual identity? Are you as concerned about the sins of pride, disunity, gossip, slander, and family neglect—in your own life and in the lives of people around you—as you are about sexual sin?
- Can we afford to let the attack against religious freedom continue unopposed?

6

Speaking Truth with Love

"Love the Lord your God with all your heart and with all your soul and with all your strength and with all your mind"; and, "Love your neighbor as yourself."

—JESUS, LUKE 10:27

For a number of years, Janet and I lived next door to Devin and Mark, two gay men.[1] In case you missed it, Janet and I are both conservative, evangelical Christians who believe all sixty-six books of the Bible are the inspired Word of God. She graduated from a Bible college and I graduated from both a Christian graduate school and seminary. We believe that the only sexual activity condoned in the Bible is that between one man and one woman in the context of marriage.[2] One form of sexual activity outside this biblical boundary is not worse than another. All sexual activity outside of biblical marriage is referred to in the Bible as "sexual immorality."[3]

The point here is that Devin and Mark obviously did not share our views on marriage and sexual immorality. Each told us of his love for the other, and they have lived together for many years. Our differences of opinion, and our friendship, opened the door for a strangely beautiful, God-ordained collision that neither Devin and Mark, nor Janet and I, will ever forget. My prayer is that you won't easily forget it either. My prayer is that in sharing this story, we all learn what it looks like to stand for truth with love and compassion. My hope is that it will help us remember that we can disagree with people on multiple levels—and even express our disagreement deeply, with crystal clarity—but do so in a kind, loving, and courteous manner that honors both God and people with whom we may have differences.

Having spent a good deal of time together as neighbors, we developed a genuine friendship with Devin and Mark, who knew that I was a pastor. One day Devin called me, saying that he and Mark wanted to adopt two needy children. The mother had died tragically, and the father was AWOL. (The children, as a result, were not getting the love and affection they deserved and needed, which Devin and Mark were ready and willing to provide.) To them, adoption seemed to be a wonderful solution to the problems these two young children faced. They wanted to know if I, as a pastor, would come to their home and pray over them, asking for God's blessing on their pursuit to adopt the children.

Janet and I talked before we walked across our yard and through their front door. We prayed. We even agonized. We genuinely loved Devin and Mark. We still do—deeply. We had laughed together, shared meals with one another, and truly enjoyed one another's company more frequently than anyone else in our community.

Janet and I also love Jesus. We seek to practice what Jesus preached because we believe it's not possible to love him without following his teachings. We also did not want to offend Devin and Mark, our friends. We knew, however, that all through the years of developing our friendship with them, the day might come when our friendship and love would be tested by having to explain our view on marriage and the family. With Devin's phone call, that day had finally arrived.

As neighbors, this was not a situation we could afford to mess up. While Janet and I walked across our yard, we kept Paul's words about "speaking the truth in love" (Eph. 4:15) in our hearts. Our aim was to not do one without the other. We intended to do both and to leave the consequences with God.

Left on my own, I am a coward. Inspired by God's Word and empowered by the Holy Spirit, I can, however, do what I would otherwise not do, go where I would otherwise not go, and say what I would otherwise not say. It's a good thing, too, because I'm far too prone to be a Peter, ready to completely deny Jesus when surveying the circumstances and relying on my own strength.[4] Can you identify?

We were warmly greeted by Devin and Mark and welcomed into the very same kitchen where we had spent time laughing and eating together on multiple occasions. There, the men explained the situation in greater detail—and their selfless desire to adopt the two children who had nowhere immediately healthy to go. We were cut to the heart by their humility and their selfless love for the children. Their hearts and stance were obvious and contagious. Oh, that more parents would express that kind of love and concern for their own children, let alone those they wished to adopt! Oh, that more heterosexual Christian couples would demonstrate the same kind of loving concern for each other that Devin and Mark displayed then, and still display, to this day.

The moment of truth—and love—did not wait long for its chance. "Mikey," Devin began, "what do you think?"

"Well . . . ," I began with a pause. *Lord, please guide my every word,* I prayed again in my heart. I knew that Janet, standing right beside me, was praying that God would give us the words that would honor both him and our love for Devin and Mark.

"I think we know what you think," interjected Mark. He then burst out with nervous laughter, saying, "But we want to know anyway!" The room grew pregnant with anticipation of what the conservative, evangelical, Bible-believing pastor would say.

"I think you know that we love you," I began softly.

"Yes," they both said softly, nodding their heads, with Mark adding, "Yes, Mike, we *know* you guys love us."

I then started to recount our times together over the years—how we had laughed and talked for great lengths at a time, helping one another in times of need that resulted in the development of a true and lasting friendship. It became unnecessary to say very much because they didn't need to be convinced. Our actions over the years were more valuable than any words would have expressed at that moment.

I then briefly explained the biblical definition of marriage and said that while I could not in good conscience bless them as a couple, I certainly could bless and pray for them individually. Guess what happened? We embraced one another, and I prayed for each individually. And I prayed for the children.

To this day, the only thing hindering our friendship is the miles that separate us. Whenever we've gone back to their city, we've rung them up and gotten together with them, even if briefly. We embrace and affirm our love for one another—because we genuinely love one another, even though we disagree about something as fundamental as marriage and sexuality.[5]

Truth and Love = Courage

It absolutely *is* possible to love someone while disagreeing with him or her. In fact, isn't this what Jesus did—as a matter of perpetual practice? Romans 5:8 says "But God demonstrates his own love for us in this: While we were still sinners, Christ died for us." Why is it that we can't get this through our thick, theologically astute skulls? God loved us—and reached out to us—not after we got our act together, but when we didn't even realize our act needed cleaning up.

> It absolutely *is* possible to love someone while disagreeing with him or her. In fact, isn't this what Jesus did—as a matter of perpetual practice?

As much as we believe all the truths of the Bible, Janet and I also believe in the need for a divine marriage between truth and love. This, too, is a biblical necessity. We believe that in order to follow in the footsteps of Jesus, such a marriage is not just important, but impossible to ignore.

Speaking the truth in love is another way of demonstrating courageous humility. It's about learning to *really* love people even when we disagree—because all people are created in the image of God. This does not mean that loving people who disagree with us condones their behaviors. If that were true, then Jesus would have been sinning by repeatedly putting himself in the presence of the unrighteous. But Jesus didn't do that. He never sinned.

Loving people involves far more than merely winning a philosophical argument and proving—or legislating—a point of view. It's true for all parties in disagreement. Courageous humility demonstrates the kind of unconditional love that reaches out to people who are very different from us, even when we know they may never change. Until we love this way, our love is not yet mature.

Speak the truth at all times—but do so with genuine humility and unmistakable love. Words spoken otherwise can become bitter pills we may one day have to swallow. Speak this way as a Christ-follower, because that is the way Jesus spoke to people every single time he addressed their sins. When we speak this way, we do Jesus proud.

Jesus is our example. He embodies what it means to speak the truth in love. He was a friend of tax collectors and sinners. Where are your tax collectors and sinners? We must have them in our lives if Jesus is our life.

To disagree with someone is not to be a hater if we speak the truth in genuine love. People know when we really love them. They can sense it. And they can sense it when all we care about is persuading them to adopt our opinion, even if our opinion is the truth. One of the greatest needs among Bible-believing Christians in America is for deep repentance for loving only the truth and not the people who need to hear it. The approach of many, ironically, has often been lacking and very unbiblical. Many of us need to ask God to (re)ignite our love for all people, recognizing that it was God's love for us that led Jesus to the cross in the first place.

To this day, Janet and I remain close friends with Devin and Mark, and we hope our friendship only grows as we age, giving us more and more opportunities to speak and live the truth in love. We don't condone Devin and Mark's lifestyle, and they don't hold our views against us. We genuinely love one another, and realize that hate is far more painful than love and that to disagree is not to hate. It is, simply, to disagree.

Love and Hatred

The definitive display of love for sinners and hatred for sin was made on the cross, where Jesus hung for your sin and mine. We cannot understand the love of God without facing our sins. We cannot look sin in the eye without peering into the eyes of Love.

At the cross we find the magnetic love of God, courtesy of the One whose practice was to spend time not with the up-and-up but the down-and-out.[6] Many of us self-professing Christ-followers today would be thrown totally off our game if Jesus returned and we were challenged to go with him to the places where real ministry and love for God are manifest. But when we really follow Christ, we'll go where he goes, do what he does, and gain his heart in the process. To reach its destination, a boat must leave the dock. It is no different from our process of maturing in Christlike love.

We Christians must have the courageous humility to call out hateful behaviors when we see them within our own ranks, reminding one another of Paul's words about "speaking the truth in love" (Eph. 4:15). Equal parts are essential in the divine recipe. If we attempt to do one without the other, we are selling out, misrepresenting the Lord who gives us this timeless command.

Transgender Love

It was the Monday after a local television news station interviewed me on my views about President Barack Obama's transgender locker-room "decree." In the interview I expressed my view that locker rooms and bathrooms should be used in accordance with one's biological sex rather than mental self-identification. The president of a local transgender rights group saw the interview and called the church to schedule a personal meeting with me. As you can imagine, I was unsure about whether the meeting would be hostile, cordial, or somewhere in between. It became obvious that he was also unsure about how I would respond to his pushback over my comments.

Our church secretary notified me that he had arrived—with a companion. Walking into the lobby, I saw a sight that looked completely ordinary—until we began to introduce one another a moment later, in my office. It was then that I learned the president, a middle-aged individual with a man's voice and a full, graying beard, identified—at times—as a woman. On that particular day, he explained, he identified as a man. His friend, a middle-aged individual with a slight build and auburn hair, was born with male genitalia, but had undergone a sex-change operation.

"Thank you for taking the time to meet with us," began John. "This is Gina,"[7] he continued, "and we are both transgender." They both explained how they had seen my interview and were, like me, concerned about President Obama's transgender decree that required all public schools, under threat of losing federal funds, to allow students to use locker rooms, showers, and restrooms in accordance with however they self-identified sexually. John and Gina explained that they did not think President Obama's actions were safe or helpful for the transgender community—that his decree would expose many transgender students to painful and unnecessary verbal and physical abuse. They explained that many within the transgender community shared the same concern but didn't know what they could do about it.

Their comments were, for a moment, a refreshing educational experience for me, as many in the media have portrayed only the most radical transgender views, leaving the majority of us little opportunity to find the common ground right beneath our own feet. Recognizing that both of them were created in the image of God just as much as I was, I thanked them for taking the time to meet and wanted to know how I could help them. They wanted to meet and educate me about what they thought were my misgivings about what constitutes transgenderism. They explained that being transgender, in their view, is a matter of the mind, not biology. John explained that he switches from being male to female in his own mind, and that he had no control over when the switch happens, or how long it lasts.

"I realize you and I may not agree on what makes someone a man or a woman," I said kindly. "I am not sure we will ever agree on that, but I respect your right to disagree, and I want you to know that I think it's possible to have a strong disagreement and to have it with love and kindness." My response was a clearly surprising alternative to the stereotypical one they thought I would display.

"You're not at all what I thought you'd be," said Gina. "You're very kind and polite, and we didn't expect that," she concluded. Her words were among the deepest compliments I could ever expect to receive from someone with whom I have a deep disagreement. They meant that I was able to communicate a stark difference of opinion in a manner that did not compromise on my love and respect for them as people loved by God and no less important to him than I am, a mere pastor.

Seeing the opportunity for common ground, I presented what I believed to be a reasonable, commonsense solution to the president's decree: require public school locker rooms, showers, and bathrooms to be used by people who share the same anatomical makeup. If a student were uncomfortable using any of these areas for any reason, schools could provide private rooms for students. I shared my view that the reason why a student wanted to use a private room need not be announced to the world. (Indeed, a student may simply have a legitimate phobia of changing in front of others.) We need not exacerbate the issue further by insisting the student disrobe around others. The entire issue could remain a private matter, and we could all function with tact and diplomacy.

My hope was that we would make joint appearances to the local school boards, demonstrating our common concern for bullying (because bullying is always wrong) and our desire that the topics of sex and sexuality be handled discreetly, without drawing undue attention to an exceptionally sensitive subject in the public school system. (Must we teach *everything* in school? I don't think so.) My idea caught traction for a moment, and it looked like we would form an unusual alliance that prevented bullying and offered a commonsense solution to a very polarizing debate in an increasingly nonsensical nation.

We have not yet been able to form the limited alliance I believe would be helpful for many to see—that foes can be friendly and that common ground can be found when we seek to love God by how we treat one another. But I'm not going to give up. Respect begins with putting ourselves in the shoes of others—but it also requires we respect not merely mortals but also the Immortal. I could not compromise on what I firmly believe the Bible teaches about sex and sexuality, that being a man or a woman is clearly determined—in the overwhelming majority of instances—by the X and Y chromosomal makeup of an individual, as designed by our Creator. A man or woman might attempt to change his or her appearance to identify in the mind differently from how he or she may present biologically, but that cannot change that person's genetic composition, which is determined solely by God.

I believe it is absolutely possible to hold firm to this position without compromise, while all along being kind and loving toward those whose views may differ. Others may have a right to express a differing view—but those of us who embrace the historic, Judeo-Christian teachings about sexuality have a humble, holy obligation to stand up and speak out to ensure that young minds and future generations do not drift from thinking that aligns with that of our Architect, who made us "male and female," to his liking (Gen. 1:27), in accordance with his very image. That image is not one you or I should tamper with. When others do, we must recognize it as the distortion it is—but we must do so with tremendous love and respect for people who, for whatever reason, do not agree with us.

Before we move into a new chapter, I think it's appropriate to pause and think deeply about two of the most popular Bible passages that address this very issue. The first is from Jesus; the second is from the apostle Paul:

> One of the teachers of the law came and heard them debating. Noticing that Jesus had given them a good answer, he asked him, "Of all the commandments, which is the most important?"
>
> "The most important one," answered Jesus, "is this: 'Hear, O Israel: The Lord our God, the Lord is one. Love the Lord your God with all your heart and with all your soul and with all your mind and with all your strength.' The second is this: 'Love your neighbor as yourself.' *There is no commandment greater than these.*"
>
> —MARK 12:28–31, EMPHASIS ADDED

> If I speak in the tongues of men or of angels, but do not have love, I am only a resounding gong or a clanging cymbal. If I have the gift of prophecy and can fathom all mysteries and all knowledge, and if I have a faith that can move mountains, but do not have love, I am nothing. If I give all I possess to the poor and give over my body to hardship that I may boast, but do not have love, I gain nothing.
>
> Love is patient, love is kind. It does not envy, it does not boast, it is not proud. It does not dishonor others, it is not self-seeking, it is not easily angered, it keeps no record of wrongs. Love does not delight in evil but rejoices with the truth. It always protects, always trusts, always hopes, always perseveres.
>
> Love never fails.
>
> —1 COR. 13:1–8

Have you given up on loving people? If you have, you've given up on loving God. Now is a great time to (re)dedicate yourself to expressing your love for God by truly, deeply, loving people.

IN A NUTSHELL

COURAGEOUS HUMILITY IN ACTION

Practical Things You Can Ponder and Practice Right Now

- Speaking the truth in love is another way of demonstrating humble courage. Being kind to someone who disagrees with you does not mean you necessarily approve of that person's behavior. It can simply communicate that you love that person with God's love while disagreeing with his or her perspective or behavior.
- To disagree with someone is not to be a hater if we speak the truth in genuine love. Jesus did this all the time.
- The cross is God's ultimate statement of hatred for sin and love for the sinner. We do well when we make the same distinction and treat people accordingly.
- One of the greatest needs among Bible-believing Christians in America is for deep repentance for loving only the truth and not the people who need to hear it. Do you have a reputation for merely speaking the truth, or for speaking the truth with authentic love?
- Jesus teaches that it's not possible to love God without loving people (see Mark 12:28–31). If we struggle with loving people, it's symptomatic of a deeper issue: loving God. What is your attitude toward people broadcasting to God about your love for him?
- Jesus was a friend of tax collectors and sinners. Are you?

7

Did Jesus Judge?

In a time of deceit, telling the
truth is a revolutionary act.

—GEORGE ORWELL

You may have heard it said that Jesus didn't judge. You may have even said that yourself. In reality, Jesus most certainly judged—*continually*. He still does, and one day every one of us will all appear before him—to be judged. Believers in Christ appear for a judgment of rewards. This is known as the "judgment seat" of Christ (Rom. 14:10; 2 Cor. 5:10). Unbelievers will be judged at the "great white throne" spoken of in Revelation 20:11–15. The white throne of judgment is not a judgment of rewards, because there is no reward for those who reject Christ. It is a judgment of eternal separation known as the "second death." A simplified way to understand the great white throne of judgment is that people who go through this life willingly rejecting God will have their desire granted, eternally, at the great white throne of judgment.

The Bible presents right and wrong, good and evil. If Jesus didn't judge, he wouldn't have given us the Bible—the Bible from which he taught. If Jesus didn't expect us to judge one another, then he would not have called anyone to teach or preach about him. We wouldn't even be able to read the Bible and judge (evaluate) ourselves, let alone others. If judgment weren't part of the Christian turf, God would not have used human beings to plant a single church, where the Bible is to be taught, embraced, and applied.

There is no getting over the fact that God chose mortal messengers to communicate the message of the Bible. Accordingly, if we believe the Bible is God's Word, we cannot help but judge everyone and everything through its lens, beginning with ourselves.

In the Great Commission, Jesus says:

> Therefore go and make disciples of all nations, baptizing them in the name of the Father and of the Son and of the Holy Spirit, and teaching them to obey everything I have commanded you. And surely I am with you always, to the very end of the age. (Matt. 28:19–20)

Notice the words *obey everything*. If there is no difference between obeying and disobeying, then what's the point? If any and every kind of attitude or behavior were acceptable to God, then how would it be possible to make a distinction between obedience and disobedience? The very notion of obedience clarifies that there are right and wrong kinds of attitudes and behaviors in the sight of God. In other words, God does judge. Jesus judges all the time. A conclusion to the contrary is more akin to a delusion.

True Love

When asked for his view of the greatest of all commandments, Jesus married love for God with love for people by quoting the Old Testament:

> "Love the Lord your God with all your heart and with all your soul and with all your mind and with all your strength." The second is this: "Love your neighbor as yourself." (Mark 12:30–31)

The surest way to assess our relationship with God is by evaluating our relationships with people. If we want to become proficient in loving him, we must master the increasingly lost art of loving one another. One of the most practical ways to do this is to develop our conflict resolution skills. Sorely lacking in today's intolerant world, conflict resolution skills will help anyone rise above the smoke and ensure that love remains the supreme pursuit in life, with increasing momentum.

When speaking about the time just before his return, the Lord said, "Because of the increase of wickedness, the love of most will grow cold" (Matt. 24:12). Jesus calls his followers to stand out, not blend in. A real Christ-follower must live and behave as a minority in a majority world. While the world is getting colder, real Christians must be on fire for God.

I love what William Booth, founder of the Salvation Army, allegedly said: "The tendency of fire is to go out. Therefore, watch the fire on the altar of your heart." The way we turn up our own heat for God and maintain our spiritual fervor for him is to continually go where Jesus went for the truths he taught—and still teaches.

The Old Testament was Jesus' continual go-to for truth. You may even be surprised to discover the Old Testament source of his teaching in Mark 12:30–31 about the greatest commandment. It comes from Deuteronomy 6:4–5 and Leviticus 19:18.

The full text of Leviticus 19:18 is worth presenting here, because that book, in particular, often gets a bum rap these days:

> Do not seek revenge or bear a grudge against anyone among your people, but love your neighbor as yourself. I am the LORD.

This is a great verse to spare you from getting into a grudge match. Even a book like Leviticus, which many people want to dismiss wholesale as being outdated and irrelevant, has timeless, practical truths. If you're rich, poor, male, female, black, white, or any color in between, God's Word makes sense. It can spare us from nonsense, because it was written by the Architect of Life.

Seeing Red?

People who think only the red letters of the New Testament contain the teachings of Jesus may be sincere, but they are sincerely wrong. When people wryly say, "Jesus didn't say that," and point to a moral teaching of the Old Testament that is up for grabs in today's relativistic society, thinking it no longer applies, they disclose that they really aren't at all familiar with Jesus or his teachings. Jesus even went so far as to say this:

> For truly I tell you, until heaven and earth disappear, not the smallest letter, not the least stroke of a pen, will by any means disappear from the Law until everything is accomplished. (Matt. 5:18)

In other words, Jesus was affirming the unchangeable importance of the Old Testament. Of course there are certain ceremonial aspects of the Old Testament law that no longer apply. (Christians do not, for instance, offer animal sacrifices.) But to dismiss the moral teachings of the Old Testament is to make a biblical blunder that cannot be resolved with the heart of God, who demonstrates a burning desire for the pinnacle of his creation—us mortals—to get along marvelously.

When we really study the Bible, we learn that all sixty-six books deal with morality and relationships. Not one book is exempt. Relationships and morality matter to God, and they must matter to his followers. This is where the subject of judging cannot help but come into focus in light of what we are witnessing in the world. How do we speak about moral and social ills if doing so is considered to be an intrusion on someone's personal rights—especially when Bible-reading Christians who truly love God and want his best can see the truth contained in 1 Corinthians 10:23:

Silence in the face of evil is the purest form of hatred.

> "I have the right to do anything," you say—but not everything is beneficial. "I have the right to do anything"—but not everything is constructive.

Truth and love must always travel together, and you and I are the ones who determine whether or not they will. It's not only what we say but often how we say things that matter to God—and deeply affect how people will receive what we have to say:

> Speaking the truth in love, we will grow to become in every respect the mature body of him who is the head, that is, Christ. (Eph. 4:15)

Not all beliefs and behaviors are beneficial to society, even if they feel good or are growing in acceptance. Christians must, if they are really following the biblical Jesus and really care about people and society, stand up and speak out. Doing so takes not only the truth but also the ability to deliver the truth with love. To not speak the truth is to not love at all. It is, in fact, to hate. Silence in the face of evil is the purest form of hatred.

The Courage to Love

To judge, biblically, is to confront sin. There is no way around it. It takes courage—and true humility. It must be done properly, or not done at all. Once again, courageous humility walks in and saves the day. Jesus says, "First take the plank out of your own eye, and then you will see clearly to remove the speck from your brother's eye" (Matt. 7:5). He did not say forget about your brother's speck and mind your own business. When we deal with our own sin (which requires humble courage), we gain the moral and spiritual authority to help others deal with theirs. Moreover, we have a moral and spiritual responsibility before God to do so, for which we will be judged. Proverbs 14:12 says, "There is a way that appears to be right, but in the end it leads to death." How can we truly love people, and God, if we don't care if they embrace death rather than the Author of Life (Acts 3:15)?

> To judge, biblically, is to confront sin. There is no way around it. It takes courage—*and true humility*. It must be done properly, or not done at all.

When we deal courageously and humbly with our own offenses against God, then, and only then, do we gain the necessary platform we need to help others find the freedom that comes from humbling themselves before Jesus and courageously following him as a result.

If we are going to handle the real haters and the reverse intolerance of those who hate Christians and Judeo-Christian values, we must remember that there was a time when we hated God and all he stands for. We just didn't realize it. Until we accepted Christ, each of us rejected him. One of the great needs among Christians today is to learn how to lovingly confront sin in healthy, biblical, godly ways. It can never be done with a Holy Roller attitude. It can only be done with humble courage that enables us to speak the truth—in love.

It's important not to ignore societal sin, and Christians are God's agents to address it; first in their own lives and then in the lives of others. First Corinthians 5:6 reminds us that "a little yeast leavens the whole batch of dough." Small sins, unconfronted, grow into diabolical debacles. "Sin, when it is full-grown, gives birth to death," says James 1:15. If we care about our culture, we must care about sin—and we must judge it. If we don't, God will judge us, along with the culture.

How to Handle the Love Haters: Dealing with #ReverseIntolerance

Now comes the part that many of us Christians confuse, distort, or botch. We point to passages where Jesus overturned the tables of the money changers, and when he rebuked the Pharisees, calling them "whitewashed tombs, which look beautiful on the outside but on the inside are full of the bones of the dead and everything unclean" (Matt. 23:27). We recount how God destroyed Sodom and Gomorrah. But we forget a truth that should be obvious: *neither you nor I are God.* We are fallen mortals, prone to wander, and prone to drop the ball far more than we pick it up.

The same God who condemned Sodom stooped with kindness toward a wayward woman (John 8:11). Let's not forget, in mentioning this, that Jesus did judge her by saying, "Go now and leave your life of sin." He did *not* approve of her lifestyle. Her pardon was genuine, her need for repentance essential. Elsewhere Jesus says, "Produce fruit in keeping with repentance" (Matt. 3:8). In Acts 26:20, the apostle Paul says, "I preached that they should repent and turn to God and *demonstrate* their repentance by their deeds" (emphasis added). Quoting Psalm 34:12–14, 1 Peter 3:10–11 says, "'Whoever would love life and see good days must keep their tongue from evil and their lips from deceitful speech. They must turn from evil and do good; they must seek peace and pursue it.'"

Repentance is not just important when it comes to following God. It is imperative.

Repentance is not just a teaching within the Bible; it is central to everything the Bible teaches. Repentance is not just important when it comes to following God. It is imperative. It is impossible to study the Bible, or to follow God, without quickly and repeatedly coming face-to-face with God's requirement that everyone who wants to follow him must change from the inside out.

With this in mind, a lot more humility in *how* we handle our own repentance, and how we approach the wayward, would go a very long way in our quest to gain their attention and positively change society. The greater our humility—the deeper and more genuine our repentance—the greater our chances are of advancing God's agenda. Without humility, we aren't going anywhere productive, with God or people. Humility is the grease of life.

Here, the words of the apostle Peter, who learned a thing or two about peer pressure, can spare us from becoming self-righteous fools who drive people away:

> But in your hearts revere Christ as Lord. Always be prepared to give an answer to everyone who asks you to give the reason for the hope that you have. But do this with gentleness and respect, keeping a clear conscience, so that those who speak maliciously against your good behavior in Christ may be ashamed of their slander. For it is better, if it is God's will, to suffer for doing good than for doing evil. (1 Peter 3:15–17)

If you are persecuted, please make sure it really is for the sake of the gospel and not because you're obnoxious, insensitive, or self-righteous. Don't confuse how you are representing Jesus and the gospel with Jesus and the gospel. In far too many instances, a lot of Christians are not getting criticized for their biblical views but for their pride and ungodly approach to confronting sin and expressing disagreements. If people criticize us, we must make sure it's for our faith, not for an ironically ungodly approach to expressing our views or even sharing the truth in arrogant, unloving ways.

Far too few of us heed Peter's Spirit-filled appeal to be prepared not merely with the words we use but also with our delivery. We must be characterized by gentleness and respect. For the Christian, it's not just the Good News that matters. It's also the manner in which we deliver the goods. Peter doesn't say we are to refrain from addressing sin. This is not an appeal to back down when we see it. It is, however, an appeal to ensure that we do some heart work in the way we address the hard work of calling out sin.

How are you doing as God's messenger of truth when you face a love hater? Can someone speak ill of you for the ways in which you confront them? If so, it's time to be courageous enough to confront yourself so your confrontations of others become *characteristically* Spirit-filled, leading people to be ashamed of their own sin to the point of their own repentance. To bully proof your life, make sure you handle sinners—even the extreme love haters—with the kind of humility befitting broken vessels such as ourselves.

Will you always confront sin correctly, with 100 percent consistency? Of course not. Only Jesus did. If you're like me, you can grow much more in the area of humility so that when the time to call out sin arrives, you can stand and deliver the Good News with *humble* courage, for God's glory.

Titanic Turmoil

Consider the book of Galatians, which depicts a titanic battle between the apostle Paul and the apostle Peter over the issue of faith and works. Once again, Peter was surrendering to peer pressure rather than God. (Can't we all identify?) His people-pleasing propensity was achieving the exact opposite of the Christian calling. Rather than leading people toward God, Peter was leading them astray. If this is possible for an apostle, how much more possible is it for you and me?

We must always be watchful to ensure that we don't compromise theological truth to placate people, and in the process lead people astray. This will always be the result when we don't spend quality time in God's Word. The words of John Bunyan should inspire us. In speaking of the Bible, he said, "This book will keep you from sin, or sin will keep you from this book."[1] If you want the fruit of the Spirit manifest in your life—and lots of it—you must frequently apply the fertilizer of Christ's Word, the Bible, to the garden of your heart and mind. Do what Colossians 3:16 says:

> Let the message of Christ dwell among you richly as you teach and admonish one another with all wisdom through psalms, hymns, and songs from the Spirit, singing to God with gratitude in your hearts.

Though Paul and Peter disagreed (Paul was in the right; Peter was deeply sinning), they agreed on how to handle sin and sinners. Both knew the power of sin and their own need for the moment-by-moment rescuing power that only the Lord Jesus can deliver.[2] Accordingly, Paul said this in the very same book where he recounted his confrontation of Peter:

> Brothers and sisters, if someone is caught in a sin, you who live by the Spirit should restore that person gently. But watch yourselves, or you also may be tempted. (Gal. 6:1)

There are times when people need to be directly confronted, as Peter needed to be, because failing to do so will result in people remaining, or becoming more entrenched, in sin. But Paul, in confronting Peter, stuck to the facts of the faith. He did not resort to name-calling or derogatory behavior, or allow theological disagreement to decay into a personal shouting match.

Do your behaviors, as someone who claims to be following Christ, reveal that you are following him closely or from a distance? Learn to model the way Paul and Peter confronted genuine sin and sinners when it was clearly needed. Let the Spirit lead. Don't let your flesh get in the way.

Morality, Manners, and Maturity

It was a sign of spiritual maturity that Paul emphasized the marriage of strong theology with loving affection. The end result was gentle, uncompromising, irresistible persuasion. This is what leads people to Christ, rather than away. When gentle persuasion is manifest in our lives, it is a sign of spiritual maturity, that humble courage has gained the higher ground and we are following Jesus more than the culture—and even more than ourselves.

Is your life characterized by mature, courageously humble behavior when confronting someone about sin? Paul is not telling us to back down when we see sin—we are indeed to call out sin. But, again, it's the manner in which we do this that makes all the difference in the world and in the lives of those being confronted.

Again, in 2 Timothy 2:25–26, Paul said this about dealing with difficult, sin-filled people:

> Opponents must be gently instructed, in the hope that God will grant them repentance leading them to a knowledge of the truth, and that they will come to their senses and escape from the trap of the devil, who has taken them captive to do his will.

The job of Christ-followers is to mature in Christ and represent him well. Our job is to call out sin when we see it. We must not compromise on this calling. But the work of the Spirit must be worked out in our own lives through a careful, prayerful, ongoing examination of our hearts, our motives, and our methods. To walk with God is to adopt a lifestyle of personal repentance. Without this, we not only lose our witness but also the chance that people will realize their sin, repent, and turn to God.

It's amazing that by the time Paul penned these words, he had learned some very deep lessons about the persuasive power that is alone found in Jesus Christ. Early in his Christian life, Paul may have had a problem knowing how to reconcile serious relational differences. He and Barnabas had such a serious falling out over what Paul saw as spiritual weakness in Mark that they parted ways. Some speculate that Paul grew considerably in this area—or should we say that God matured Paul? The same Mark that caused him consternation years earlier was later referred to by Paul: "Get Mark and bring him with you, because he is helpful to me in my ministry" (2 Tim. 4:11).

Something beautiful happened in Paul's life as he walked more and more closely with Jesus. The Jesus he had been preaching so thoroughly saturated who he was that he began to resemble him more and more. The same will be true of you and me, when we truly humble ourselves before God and give Jesus our all. Yes, Jesus judged—and so must you if you are going to follow him. Just make sure you pass judgment with real humility, in the overflow of your own loving obedience to God.

IN A NUTSHELL

COURAGEOUS HUMILITY IN ACTION

Practical Things You Can Ponder and Practice Right Now

- Have you believed the lie that Jesus didn't—and doesn't—judge?
- It's not possible to love God without judging and confronting sin. When confronting it in ourselves, we must be relentless. When confronting it in others, we must be humble.
- The Bible is the ultimate guide for human relationships. If you regularly read the Bible, you'll be in a position to put its teachings into practice. If you want the fruit of the Spirit manifest in your life—and lots of it—you must frequently apply the fertilizer of Christ's Word, the Bible, to the garden of your heart and mind.
- It's not that we read the Bible that makes a difference, but it's how we read it. Do you have a set time each day,

when you look at the Bible and ask God to teach you, through it, how to treat people? Do you constantly look for ways throughout your day to apply the Bible you know?

- Have you lost (or never had) your moral and spiritual platform to speak into the lives of others because you've failed to remove the log of sin from your own eye? Why not ask God to help you with your sin so you can help others with theirs?

8

The Present Future

Mind Control and Thought Police

> We are fast approaching the stage of the ultimate inversion: the stage where the government is free to do anything it pleases, while the citizens may act only by permission; which is the stage of the darkest periods of human history, the stage of rule by brute force.
>
> —AYN RAND

I think it's a good practice for every pastor and educator to prepare for and deliver every message as if it were his or her last.[1] I try to take my own advice, and the message I had just given was no exception. I had just poured myself out, holding nothing back in the last of a series of messages to a group of faculty and students preparing for careers as pastors, educators, and missionaries at a well-known Bible school. I was speaking about the need for humble courage in today's world of arrogant fear, trying to encourage these future leaders to take their faith, and the perfect convergence of America's problems, seriously. One of the things I addressed was how apathy and fatalism (disguised as faith) among Christians and Christian leaders, if not reversed, is going to guarantee real persecution, not merely discomfort, for people of faith.

It was a young crowd, and I wanted the students to not merely sit and listen, but to be able to ask questions and be heard. It wasn't long before the question I anticipated was raised: "You know, the church in other countries—where Christians are *really* being persecuted—is growing in leaps and bounds. Don't you think the church in America could benefit from a little persecution? In fact, we know that the apostle Paul's imprisonment was something God used to advance, not hinder, the gospel." (See Paul's testimony in Philippians 1:12–14.) This question is outstanding, and I'm glad it was asked not only for the benefit of the audience at hand but now, also, for the wider audience of Christians who are reading this book and sharing it with friends.

The kind of question raised by the student often initially throws cold water on any warm discussion regarding the need for Christian courage, because it's hard to argue with the truth of Scripture: God *did* use Paul's imprisonment to advance the gospel. In fact, it is no exaggeration to say that were it not for his imprisonment, the faith of many would not have been built up as a direct result. *Upon closer examination, however, the question (and the point it seeks to support) does nothing to justify the sins of indifference, laziness, and fatalism.* Just because God uses persecution to advance his cause doesn't mean we should tempt him to use it because of our own lethargy.

Many Christians have mistaken fatalism for faith. Fatalism and faith are foes, not friends. Without realizing it, many American Christians are already conceding defeat, voluntarily surrendering our rights to free speech, religion, and press as if there were no other option. Many of us pastors and Christian leaders are the biggest culprits. In so doing, we are creating a self-fulfilling prophecy about our own demise by confusing the sovereignty of God with Christian responsibility. If God is sovereign in persecution, why can't he be sovereign in freedom?

It's our lack of passion for God, in the end, not a persecuting government, that results in our witness for Christ being diminished in America. Let's not fantasize about religious persecution while we neglect our responsibility to do all we can to protect freedom so that the gospel can be proclaimed without it. It is a subtle sin—but a diabolical one nonetheless—to care little about freedom when all it would take to preserve it is a little bit of biblical backbone.

At this moment Christians in persecuted countries, who are being *severely* persecuted for their faith, are in a very different place than American Christians are today. While they have already lost their religious freedoms, we have not yet come to that point. We most certainly will, however, if we allow ourselves to embrace the escapist mentality of the well-meaning Bible college student. Here, we must again be reminded that if we ignore our freedoms, they will go away. And if our religious freedom goes away for no reason other than our own foolish disregard for its value, we will have to give an account before Almighty God for our negligence.

If we ignore our freedoms, they will go away.

The sin of apathetic fatalism among many Christians in America is an extremely serious one. If you're guilty of it, now is the time to ask God's forgiveness. Now is the time to ask him to ignite your life for him and change your ways—not because we face persecution, but because Jesus Christ is worthy of our absolute best.

Frog in the Kettle

In most instances, the loss of religious freedom in persecuted countries often came gradually, not overnight. It may have reached its boiling point in one decisive moment, but its onslaught was slow and steady. If we don't start to stand up consistently and unapologetically against religious persecution (which is happening in the name of creating a more tolerant America), we are hastening the day when serious religious persecution will become a permanent reality in America. Our apathetic fatalism is guaranteeing it. It is not a matter of if, but when.

Ask yourself a few of the following questions. I'm asking them in an intentionally repetitive fashion, exploring different nuances with each phrasing, to help each of us think deeply about where we are going if we allow fatalistic apathy to rule our lives while our current downward trajectory continues—if a movement of humble courage does not arise throughout the land.

- Imagine if Congress passed laws restricting the free exercise of religion because it determined that "deep-seated religious beliefs" were discriminatory, intolerant, hateful, or incompatible with what most Americans want. Imagine if justices in the circuit, federal, state supreme courts, and the Supreme Court began handing down decisions that enforced such legislation. How would that affect the "free exercise of religion" guaranteed in our First Amendment? How could that affect your ability to love and serve Jesus Christ, to teach your children how to do so, and to openly encourage others toward the same?
- Imagine if America became a nation where laws were in place that forbid you to practice or teach your religion to others. Imagine a nation where this was not just frowned upon, but

where you were forbidden—under threat of fines, imprisonment, or both—to teach deeply held religious and moral beliefs because they were deemed intolerant, hateful, discriminatory, or incompatible with government standards or a court of law. Imagine a world where teaching your own children about God could result in your being fined, imprisoned, or losing custody of your children.

- Imagine an America where parents and guardians could be forced to send their children to reorientation schools, where they would learn values completely contrary to the core convictions of their parents/guardians, including deep-seated, millennia-old religious (i.e., biblical) beliefs deemed intolerant, hateful, discriminatory, or incompatible with government standards.
- Imagine an America where it was commonplace for companies and employers to face crippling fines or the threat of closure unless they were willing to compromise deeply held religious or moral beliefs—beliefs deemed intolerant, hateful, discriminatory, or incompatible with modern culture, as determined by the government.
- Imagine an America where a pastor, rabbi, religious leader, or teacher could face financial ruin through fines and/or the threat of serving years in jail simply for teaching historic, biblical views on marriage, sex, gender, and sexuality.
- Imagine a world where a church, synagogue, or academic institution could have its assets seized or be forced to close its doors if its teachings were deemed intolerant, hateful, discriminatory, or incompatible with standards determined by the government or a court of law. (This is why Supreme Court justices, court of appeals judges, and district court judges matter so very much. This is why the president of the United States matters, because he or she gets to nominate all empty justice seats for approval by Congress.)

The reason you need to ponder the above scenarios is because they will become reality in America if people of faith allow it. If we do not arise, with courageous humility, our religious freedom will become a thing of the past.

Think About Thought Police: Muse over Mind Control

Thought police and mind control are not the things of science fiction; they are inescapable certainties wherever the free exercise of religion and speech are limited. While no government can regulate what we *now* believe about the Bible and the teachings of Jesus (deep-seated religious beliefs), if our freedom of speech were subject to government regulation, it could clearly affect what people believe—and practice—in the future. We Americans are not thinking about the importance of unhindered free speech nearly enough, and it's exactly why we are not yet standing up and speaking out as we must. You and I need to think ahead to how limits on free speech today could drastically limit the freedom of worship tomorrow.

All aspects of life are much harder without free speech. As freedom of speech goes, so goes the freedom of religion, because these two are eternally married. As freedom of speech goes, so goes the ease with which we can teach and preach the gospel. It will affect what our children learn—and don't learn. This, in turn, will affect not only what they believe and think, but also how they *live* in response to what they believe. We need to let this understanding grip us, because we do not seem to fully grasp that there is a direct relationship between what we believe and think about God, our ability to live for him, and our ability to help others do the same. Since worship has *everything* to do with pleasing God—and there is nothing more important than pleasing him—freedom of speech is really ground zero in the war against God, the gospel, and the teachings of historic, biblical Christianity.

Censorship in the name of tolerance should be a deep, courage-igniting concern for people of *all* faiths, not just Bible believers. We may be a nation of diverse faiths, but we should all agree that freedom of speech is vital for every one of us, because whoever succeeds in limiting the freedoms of press, speech, and religion will have the power to limit not only what we believe, but also how future generations think and live. Now is a good time to pause, reread that last sentence, and let it sink in deeply before you read another word.

Close Call

Let's take a brief look back at one of the most contentious presidential races in American history and revisit the year 2016. I feel I have to apologize for even bringing it up, but it's necessary because what happened in 2016 could happen during any American political campaign if people of faith remove themselves from political involvement for years. The 2016 election marked a turning point in American presidential campaigns.

While past elections afforded people of faith a chance to at least vote for a candidate who shared their values, many felt they did not even remotely have that choice in our Republican and Democratic candidates. Neither provided the real hope and change that could make our nation stronger together, great again. (I'm not even sure we ever were as great as some people think we were. Greatness is a relative term.[2] And if by promoting a nation that is stronger together it is meant that deep-seated religious beliefs need to take a backseat so we can all ride together [tolerance], we're simply setting ourselves up for a massive collision with the teachings of Jesus. Some may find hope in that, but not the kind of change that honors God.)

Here's the Monday-morning quarterback question for the 2016 election, which we need to answer properly so that what happened in 2016 does not become the new normal in America: How did we end up with what many considered to be a depressing, uninspiring, very polarizing choice of candidates?

For starters, the 2016 election didn't happen in a vacuum. It was the by-product of what happens when people of faith detach themselves and give in to apathy over many years. It's what happens when people of faith fail to act over the long haul—not simply during an election year, but in the years leading up to it. I think we wound up with a "hail Mary,"[3] last gasp approach to the presidential election because, for far too long, people of faith were not humbly, attentively involved in the political process. When we lose our courage and our humble resolve to be agents of change, bad things happen: we end up with very poor political candidates. Society and culture suffer greatly.

The year 2016 was when our chickens came home to roost, when we began to reap the full force of the self-imposed political exile that we sowed for years. If we want candidates with good morals, who represent our values and the policies that best reflect our beliefs in any area of life, this outcome is best ensured by engaging in, not removing ourselves from, the political process in the years leading up to the election. We did the exact opposite leading up to 2016, and that's why we wound up where we did.

The 2016 presidential candidate pool brought the United States very close to electing a president who *openly* promoted targeting and altering religious beliefs seen as obstacles to a political agenda. In delivering a keynote address at the 2015 Women in the World Summit, the candidate made the following comment: "Deep-seated cultural codes, religious beliefs, and structural biases have to be changed."[4]

Even though the candidate was addressing deep-seated religious beliefs among Muslims, we Christians should be concerned—along with people of all faiths—because the loss of religious freedom, through legislative restrictions, could come to any religious group. Now reread the sentence from the candidate's speech but substitute the word *biblical* for the word *religious.* See how that makes a world of difference if you are a Christ-follower? What if a person's "deep-seated religious beliefs" come from the teachings of the Bible? The restriction of free speech and religion should be something about which we are all intolerant.

No government can regulate what we believe *now* about the teachings of Jesus, but if it were allowed to limit our freedom of speech, it could hinder our ability to help others believe and practice what he taught—what Jesus wants taught in perpetuity—until his return.

If deep-seated religious/biblical beliefs can be targeted for the purpose of changing what people believe, isn't that the crossing of a dangerous line? Whatever happened to separation of church and state? It does not exist—unless it becomes convenient to mention as a way to keep people of faith from standing up and speaking out when that kind of courage is exactly what is needed to protect religious freedom.

The Great Omission

No government can regulate what we believe *now* about the teachings of Jesus, but if it were allowed to limit our freedom of speech, it could hinder our ability to help others believe and practice what he taught—what Jesus wants taught in perpetuity—until his return.

If Americans elect legislators and justices are appointed who believe that deep-seated religious/biblical beliefs must be changed, legislation can be introduced and passed in order to achieve that objective. This could directly affect what is taught in public schools, the workplace, and other institutions. It could even affect homeschooling and private schools because if something is considered to be discriminatory, the government could pass legislation to restrict it.

Churches and religious institutions could, indeed, be told to stop teaching long-standing religious/biblical beliefs because those beliefs are deemed hateful by the government. People with religious/biblical views opposing those of the government could be pressured to the point of silence or perhaps face fines, imprisonment, or both—all made possible through legislation reflecting the worldview of the legislators. The end result would be exactly what the candidate envisioned: deep-seated religious/biblical beliefs would indeed be changed.

Hidden in Plain Sight

If the words *mind control* were openly used to describe what's happening in America, we'd all be instantly alarmed and resist vehemently. But this is exactly what we are allowing to take place by refusing to stand up and speak out. Mind control is the real war on terror we have yet to resist. A covert operation is cunningly underway, but most of us are AWOL in the fight because we are not paying attention. We are not thinking about the logical, immoral, godless,

Mind control is the real war on terror we have yet to resist.

imprisoned culture of reverse intolerance that we will embolden by our silence—intolerance to deep-seated biblical beliefs and the people who possess them.

We have a holy obligation before God to evaluate political parties and political candidates objectively, through the lens of Scripture. Character, policies, and political philosophies matter because they can hinder or help the agenda of Jesus Christ and the advancement of the Great Commission.

Consider Colossians 1:28–29, and think about what our aim should be as Christians living in America at this particular time, when freedom is under attack:

> He is the one we proclaim, admonishing and teaching everyone with all wisdom, *so that we may present everyone fully mature in Christ.* To this end I strenuously contend with all the energy Christ so powerfully works in me.[5]

The Christian's goal is to become a mature follower of Jesus and to help others do the same. If our government is allowed to change deep-seated religious/biblical beliefs—if we allow it to hinder our freedom to teach God's Word in any area of life—then it could directly affect even our attempts to "present everyone fully mature in Christ."

Look at 1 Timothy 2:1–6:

> I urge, then, first of all, that petitions, prayers, intercession and thanksgiving be made for all people—for kings and all those in authority, that we may live peaceful and quiet lives in all godliness and holiness. This is good, and pleases God our Savior, *who wants all people to be saved and to come to a knowledge of the truth.* For there is one God and one mediator between God and

> mankind, the man Christ Jesus, who gave himself as a ransom for all people. This has now been witnessed to at the proper time.[6]

Note the italics. It is God's will that people come to the knowledge of the truth and give their lives to Christ as Savior. A government that may seek to impose legislation that obstructs our ability to do this is not something God's people should take lying down.

Finally, let's take a serious look at Acts 5:27–29:

> The apostles were brought in and made to appear before the Sanhedrin to be questioned by the high priest. "We gave you strict orders not to teach in this name," he said. "Yet you have filled Jerusalem with your teaching and are determined to make us guilty of this man's blood."
>
> Peter and the other apostles replied: "*We must obey God rather than human beings!*"[7]

It is the cry of the apostles to obey God above everything and everyone. Is this your cry too? It must be if Jesus is your master. Are *you* concerned about obeying God more than any legislator or piece of legislation that may be enacted that would prevent you from teaching others a biblical truth you know to be important? If you aren't, it could be a sign that you aren't pursuing your greatest in Christ. It would be no surprise, then, if you had little interest in seeing other people reach their greatest maturity in Christ as well.

We must care about being able to advance the kingdom of God and the will of God *with as much freedom as possible.* We must care about godliness because we should know how terrible it is to live life without it.

I know from my own failures, from time spent wallowing in the mud, how terrible it is to walk in sin. I've been in bondage for no other reason than rejecting the full teaching of Scripture—for choosing to be immature instead of mature. You may know what that's like too. It's not pretty. People need to know God's truths so they can live godly, dignified lives in *every* way and be spared from trying to live life like a pig wallowing in the mud. God's truth, and the freedom that results when we embrace it, is one key reason why the First Amendment matters. It's why freedom of the press, freedom of speech, and freedom of religion mean more than we may have realized.

Fugazy Jesus?

We *must* care about teaching people to obey *everything* Jesus commanded, because if we teach selectively about Jesus, we will end up presenting an incomplete "fugazy" Jesus—a genuine fake.[8] We must recall the words of Paul as he warned wayward believers in 2 Corinthians 11:4:

> For if someone comes and proclaims another Jesus than the one we proclaimed, or if you receive a different spirit from the one you received, or if you accept a different gospel from the one you accepted, you put up with it readily enough. (ESV)

Proclaiming "another Jesus" or receiving a "different spirit" is heretical. And this is not the only time we are given such a strong warning against doing so. In Galatians 1:8, Paul said,

> But even if we or an angel from heaven should preach to you a gospel contrary to the one we preached to you, let him be accursed. (ESV)

It's no small thing to teach selectively about Jesus. We either endeavor to teach *everything* about him or we end up with a Jesus other than the One presented in the Bible. If someone seeks to prevent us from teaching *anything* Jesus commanded, that person is a hindrance to our preaching and teaching about the real Jesus and becomes an obstacle to helping others live the kind of life that most glorifies God.

A government that can define and redefine hate speech will be able to say it promotes freedom of speech, press, and religion all day long while simultaneously destroying it. What if Congress were to pass laws restricting the free exercise of religion because they determined that "deep-seated religious beliefs" were discriminatory, intolerant, hateful, or incompatible with modern cultural standards? If our government is allowed to change deep-seated religious/biblical beliefs, then it could directly affect our ability to "present everyone fully mature in Christ," and put itself on a collision course with God.

A government that can define and redefine hate speech will be able to say it promotes freedom of speech, press, and religion all day long while simultaneously destroying it.

If any government or any person within that government—no matter what political party he or she may be part of—seeks to hinder our God-given mandate to freely teach people to observe everything Jesus commanded, to freely help people live godly lives that follow what Jesus commanded, or to freely show people how to become mature in Christ, then it is the obligation of every Christ-following man, woman, boy, and girl to obey God rather than man.

IN A NUTSHELL

COURAGEOUS HUMILITY IN ACTION

Practical Things You Can Ponder and Practice Right Now

- Imagine an America where biblical beliefs were targeted, where you were told that you could not teach your children, or your congregation, what the Bible teaches. Pay attention to any attempt to hinder the freedom of the press, speech, and religion, because if we allow these, we invite and guarantee real, potentially permanent, persecution.
- Ask God to help you understand why *maturity* in Christ, not just knowing him as Savior, is so important in loving, honoring, and worshiping him. Ask him to give you a heart to help others be mature too.
- A person whose life goal isn't to become mature in Christ won't care much about Christlike maturity developing in others. What does your concern (or lack of concern) for the ability of others to mature in Christ say about your pursuit of Jesus Christ? Are you really interested in maturing in Christ to the greatest possible degree and helping others do the same?
- When it comes to standing up and speaking out for God, keep the words of the apostles in mind, that we must obey God rather than people (Acts 5:29).

9

Broken Glass

First they came for the Socialists, and I did not speak out—
Because I was not a Socialist.
Then they came for the Trade Unionists, and I did not speak out—
Because I was not a Trade Unionist.
Then they came for the Jews, and I did not speak out—
Because I was not a Jew.
Then they came for me—and there was no one
left to speak for me.

—PASTOR MARTIN NIEMÖLLER

On November 9–10, 1938, Nazis dressed in plainclothes pounced upon unarmed German civilians, rounding up thousands of Jews and destroying Jewish property on what became known as *Kristallnacht*, the "night of broken glass." The name comes from the shattered glass carpeting the streets after Jewish-owned stores, synagogues, hospitals, and buildings were destroyed with sledgehammers by the Nazis.[1] On that night lives, not just objects, were demolished.

What happened in Germany did not come about overnight. It took years to get to the night of broken glass, the powder keg moment when the gradual transformation of the nation finally came to a breaking point. The German people first had to be reeducated about their view of Jews, then taught that the role of government was to be supreme—even over God and religion—and before they knew it, the people didn't merely tolerate what the government was doing, they welcomed it. They had been suffering from a huge leadership void and were ready and willing to have someone, *anyone*, help them regain their sense of worth, value, and greatness.

On the surface there were no concerns; after all, Hitler's leadership and policies boosted the morale of the people. The fiendish pieces had been put into place gradually, in the name of creating a better society, making it greater than it had ever before been. The people were now *willing* to be led by a cold, calculating, incredibly charismatic leader, a dynamic speaker with brazenness never before seen. The average person did not know that behind the veil, yet before their very eyes, they had been duped into thinking, acting, tolerating, and now applauding previously unthinkable, horrific attitudes and acts. The culture was successfully transformed, ready to be a well-oiled machine that would reproduce itself generation after generation. The perfect conditions now existed to accomplish what was previously inconceivable.

The apathy manifest among many Christians is exactly what is necessary for history to repeat itself.

As a Christian living in America, how keenly are you paying attention to what is happening within state and local government? Could what happened in Germany happen here—and should you, as a Christian, care? The apathy manifest among many Christians is exactly what is necessary for history to repeat itself. Here, a humility checkup is in order for every person of faith living in America. Is our apathy costing us our future freedom?

American Kristallnacht?

Something similar to Kristallnacht could happen again, not just in a foreign country, but here, in America, at any time. Before you assume that I'm out of my mind to suggest this, please bear with me as I try to explain the maneuvering that's taken place in America over recent years. A gradual, fundamental transformation has been underway, and will continue, unless many more Americans become attentive, engaged, and act with courageous humility.

All that is needed is for a persuasive president of the United States to decide that someone's words or actions are extremist or constitute hate speech. In the name of peace, tolerance, and safety, it could be determined that such a person can be detained, or perhaps relocated, in order to reduce the risk of others embracing their views—views determined to be out of step with the vision and direction of the country. It all starts with a president simply making the charge that someone—perhaps you, an American citizen—is an extremist. That's how America's Kristallnacht could begin. This could happen to you or to someone you love. It could happen to anyone who crosses the nebulous red line that has been drawn, and continues to be redrawn, here in America. Keep reading and you will see how the pieces are already in place.

Absolute power corrupts absolutely—and indiscriminately. The political pendulum swings both left and right, and the potential for the abuse of power should concern you whether you are progressive or conservative. It should definitely concern you if you are a Christian and embrace Judeo-Christian values. Freedoms of speech, religion, the press, and peaceable assembly—all protected in the

First Amendment of our Constitution and unalienable, God-given rights, as well—should matter to us to such a degree that we take objective stands to defend them when threatened. We must be nonpartisan when it comes to these vital values. If freedoms are taken from one person, they can be taken from another. Everyone suffers when freedom is attacked.

There may not be much broken glass or many demolished buildings here, at least not at first, but lives will be destroyed nonetheless. Beliefs can be dismantled, freedoms hindered, rights trampled, and lives torn apart, so that the rest of society—the weary, fed-up masses—can move on with their new vision of what America should be. Brilliantly, it will all be done in the name of creating a more peaceful, safe, tolerant, and loving society.

An American Kristallnacht is very possible—and I would argue that it is probable. Unless we adjust our lives to turn things around. Here is why:

- Most of us are exhausted, exasperated, and nearly out of gas. We're busy trying to simply make ends meet in what seems to be an exercise in economic futility. Many of us have lost jobs, or found replacement jobs that are nowhere near the rate of pay we previously enjoyed. Even two-income families are struggling.[2] Childcare and healthcare costs alone are exorbitant.
- Most of us are too distracted. We amuse and distract ourselves into oblivion through time spent surfing the Internet, watching movies and TV shows, playing electronic games, obsessing with social media, and sending texts. (The average American spends eight to ten hours a day on media devices, even more time than sleeping.)[3]
- Most of us feel a bit belittled and bullied in one way or another. We simply want *someone* to protect us.

- Most of us have grown accustomed to being told what to think and have lost the ability to think for ourselves. Constructive, critical thinking is no longer taught in the majority of schools, nor do the majority of people value it. If we see something on television, read a blog, or learn it from a press conference, we don't question the credibility of the source. We don't look for objectivity or test things for accuracy and truth. If the medium is packaged well (and in some cases even poorly), we accept it readily enough.

We are ready for leaders and policies that will murder freedom. We even seem more than ready for it. *We seem hungry.*

- The government has become our savior, our god. The government now has such an intrusive, powerful role in nearly every area of our lives and businesses that most of us have come to depend on the government more than God. The growing temptation is to believe that the government, rather than Jesus Christ, is our savior.

Now, or any time from this point on, is the perfect time to hand a crying baby a political soother, to have the American government step in as the mommy and daddy we never had. Our entire culture, the large majority of American people, is now ready, willing, and able to embrace and do what we never would have endorsed just a few years ago. We are ready for leaders and policies that will murder freedom. We even seem more than ready for it. *We seem hungry.*

It is not a mystical methodology that enables a frighteningly accurate prediction of the future. It's simply a reflection on the past, and "those who cannot remember the past are condemned to repeat it."[4] As Winston Churchill said,

> Want of foresight, unwillingness to act when action would be simple and effective, lack of clear thinking, confusion of counsel until the emergency comes, until self-preservation strikes its jarring gong—these are the features which constitute the endless repetition of history.[5]

Our want of foresight, unwillingness to act, lack of clear thinking, and confusion about what is right and wrong have primed the American pump. We've lost our moral compass. We are ready for change. Despair can now be cast as hope. Change, no matter what it looks like, can be perceived as good. Events similar to what took place in Germany, which paved the way for Kristallnacht, have already taken place here in America.

None of this is to suggest that our sitting president (or any prior presidents) can be, at this time, likened to Adolf Hitler.[6] It is to say, however, that laws have *already* been passed and steps have already been taken in America that have opened doors that never should have been opened. In so doing, those laws provide opportunities for any willing president with enough charisma and a complacent populace to do what is, at this moment, unthinkable. They provide the opportunities for history to be repeated.

There is a fitting poem that bundles up what we've been exploring here and can help us see the simplicity of what America needs. It's called "For Want of a Nail":

> *For want of a nail the shoe was lost.*
> *For want of a shoe the horse was lost.*
> *For want of a horse the rider was lost.*
> *For want of a rider the battle was lost.*
> *For want of a battle the kingdom was lost.*
> *And all for the want of a horseshoe nail.*[7]

America's "horseshoe nail" is courageous humility. It's what we're missing, and what needs to be rediscovered among Christians especially. We have a moral responsibility before God to see that tyrants do not overrun our nation. This is a concern that must be shared by conservatives and progressives. The concern of absolute power corrupting absolutely is something that should unite us behind a common cause that benefits our entire nation.

It's important for all Americans, but especially for Christians, to hold our public servants accountable, to ensure that power does not descend into corrupt power. This is one vital reason why our Constitution, which provides checks and balances of power, is important to uphold, protect, and defend—not just among government leaders, but also among us who elect them. Once we elect people, it's up to us to ensure they lead with integrity and the kind of humble courage needed to govern—but never at the risk of freedom.

While We Were Sleeping

On New Year's Eve 2011, while many Americans were too distracted, tired, or drunk to pay attention, President Barack Obama signed the National Defense Authorization Act (NDAA, S-1857).[8] The law gives the president—and all future presidents—the authority to have US citizens arrested, detained, and interrogated by the military for an indefinite period of time—without trial, legal counsel, or the whereabouts of the arrested individuals being known by anyone but the government, providing they meet the current definition of what it means to be a "terrorist."[9] Specifically, it affirms the "authority of the Armed Forces of the United States to detain covered persons pursuant to the Authorization for Use of Military Force."[10] Section 1022(a)(1) reads as follows:

> IN GENERAL.—Except as provided in paragraph (4), the Armed Forces of the United States shall hold a person described in paragraph (2) who is captured in the course of hostilities authorized by the Authorization for Use of Military Force (Public Law 107–40) in military custody pending disposition under the law of war.

But 1022(a)(4) effectively negates the above requirement, saying:

> The President may waive the requirement of paragraph (1) if the President submits to Congress a certification in writing that such a waiver is in the national security interests of the United States.

All it would take is for a president to accuse someone of being a terrorist or engaging in terror, as part of al-Qaeda or "an associated force."[11] The definitions of what constitute terror, terrorist, or terrorism can change. They already have, *multiple* times. What if they change again to include swaths of people whose views and actions could be considered to be at odds with the shifting sands of opinion and policy? What is being applied to true terrorists today could pivot and end up being used in ways that now seem unthinkable.

Before you walk away in disbelief, thinking this is the language of a conspiracy theory or fodder for a new spy thriller, before you start hammering away on your keyboard or smart device to fact-check this, slow down for a moment. Keep reading and you'll spare yourself the research. This is not fabrication. It is fact. A good number of credible, authoritative people and organizations object to the NDAA's indefinite detention provision. We would be foolish to dismiss their concerns.[12]

Even President Obama—who signed the law into effect—expressed his reservations because the NDAA's language is so vague that it makes unconstitutional government aggression easier than ever before.[13] The fact that the president expressed concern should make all of us sit up and take note of how the law is merely subject to interpretation by a sitting president, subject to a judicial interpretation only *after* it has been challenged. In other words, it is simply up to a president to determine its interpretation as he or she sees fit, and to then act, accordingly:

> I want to clarify that my administration will not authorize the indefinite military detention without trial of American citizens. Indeed, I believe that doing so would break with our most important traditions and values as a nation.[14]

President Obama's words are comforting in one sense, but very troubling in another, because the issue is far more significant than the possibility of breaking "with our most important traditions and values as a nation." It's a matter of a president potentially authorizing the detention of an American citizen in accordance with the NDAA—and in so doing, violating the Sixth Amendment to the Constitution.[15] Christians and Constitution-loving citizens, where is your concern for holding our leaders accountable?

CBS reported as follows: "Mr. Obama says his administration will interpret that provision 'in a manner that ensures that any detention it authorizes complies with the Constitution, the laws of war, and all other applicable law.'"[16] Again, this is more disturbing than comforting. The law should *already* ensure that, and not be left up to a sitting president to test by his or her actions.

What you may not realize is that while the NDAA's indefinite detention provision could be challenged in a court of law and overturned, the person doing the challenging would have to demonstrate that he or she was personally impacted by it. For instance, that person would have to have been indefinitely detained in order to challenge the law. Here is the problem: how in the world could a US citizen, arrested and detained by the US military—in an undisclosed location, without access to legal counsel—petition a court to hear his or her case? They couldn't. It would be impossible. So much for an American citizen's right to a fair and speedy trial, protected by the Sixth Amendment.

So why did the president sign this bill if it is fundamentally flawed, opening the door to the unconstitutional military incarceration of US citizens upon the whim of presidential interpretation? Why did Mr. Obama even subject our nation to such vulnerability? What if a future president does not exercise the caution that President Obama at least voiced? How could an elected legislator, sworn to uphold, protect, and defend the Constitution, introduce this bill to Congress? How in the world, considering the lengthy process of checks and balances involved in a bill becoming a law, did the bill even make it to the president's desk?

The purpose of the Constitution is to be preemptive, to protect all of us from potential tyranny. This bill invites it. Even the ACLU, a typically liberal organization, spoke out against the NDAA, saying,

> The breadth of the NDAA's worldwide detention authority violates the Constitution and international law because it is not limited to people captured in an actual armed conflict, as required by the laws of war.[17]

The ACLU failed to mention the more important issue for us Americans: how it threatens to undermine, even negate, our Constitution. Article 1, Section 9 of the Constitution (remember, our national "rudder") says this:

> The Privilege of the Writ of Habeas Corpus shall not be suspended, unless when in Cases of Rebellion or Invasion the Public Safety may require it.[18]

"Writ of habeas corpus" is Latin for "that you have the body," meaning there must be a body of evidence, a reasonable cause, to detain an American citizen. It is regularly applied in our courts (as a constitutional requirement) to ensure that the detention of a prisoner is valid while the prisoner awaits his or her right to a fair and speedy trial. In other words, the writ of habeas corpus exists to ensure that people are not indefinitely detained without evidence and are not denied due justice under the law.

The ACLU's concern about the NDAA's indefinite detention provision is completely justified. The provision makes the writ of habeas corpus irrelevant for an American citizen accused of being a terrorist, as if the writ wasn't the constitutional guarantee it is.

If you love freedom and the long-standing policies in the United States that a person is presumed innocent until proven guilty and that everyone has the right to a speedy and fair trial, the NDAA should raise more than your eyebrow. It should cause us to stand up and speak out because it significantly undermines the US Constitution.[19]

The passage of the NDAA indefinite detention provision gives the president the freedom to determine—by whatever standard he or she may choose—who may be detained and under what circumstances that US citizen may be indefinitely detained (imprisoned). American citizens are now skating on very thin ice.

Homeland Insecurity?

In 2014, I attended a gathering where our Pennsylvania congressman, Scott Perry[20] (PA-4), was the featured speaker. At the time he was a member of the House Committee for our US Department of Homeland Security (DHS), and has since become the chair of the subcommittee.[21] Like many Americans, I had heard stories of our

DHS buying up billions and billions of rounds of ammunition[22] and wanted to know if the reports were true or just the fodder of conspiracy theory alarmists circulating nonsense. To grasp the sheer volume of how long 1.6 billion rounds would last, consider that when fighting was fiercest in the Iraq War, the US Army was firing less than 6 *million* rounds a month. So 1.6 billion bullets could sustain a war with fighting as intense as that in Iraq for more than twenty years.[23] I wondered, for what kind of domestic war was the DHS preparing?

I hate nonsense and speculation; I always want *facts*. (The DHS, keep in mind, was designed not for foreign wars but for the protection of our motherland, the people who traverse the byways and highways of domestic America.)

Have our legislators created a Dr. Jekyll and Mr. Hyde situation here in our homeland, where what is now being restrained could be used without restraint or in ways that were never intended?

When the Q&A time began, I raised my hand and waited to be called upon. When acknowledged, I stood up and respectfully asked Mr. Perry if the reports of massive ammunition purchases by the DHS were true, to which he replied, "Yes." I kindly asked him why the department was making such purchases (including hollow-point ammunition, which is designed to inflict maximum damage), since the DHS's oversight was for *domestic* America. To this he replied, "I don't know." I appreciated his honesty but was shocked by the admission from a person who was on a House committee for the department.

So I asked again if he could justify why the DHS would make such a large purchase. He again replied, "I don't know." In disbelief over what appeared to be Mr. Perry's genuine lack of knowledge over the reason for the purchases, and the fact that he was serving on the DHS committee, I asked a third time, hoping for some kind of answer that would reverse the disappointing momentum of his responses. Instead, he repeated, for the third time, that he did not know why the DHS had purchased the ammunition. I sat down and dropped the issue, discouraged that an elected representative, given his position of responsibility on the committee, didn't know the answer to such a fundamental, crucial question. I turned to my friend, who had accompanied me to the meeting, and said, "We're doomed. If our own representatives who are serving on committees don't know what's going on, then who in the world is running the show?"

If an elected representative serving on the committee of the DHS does not know why the department under his oversight is taking questionable action, should we not all be concerned? What kind of mess are we Americans in if our leaders are in the dark? Who is really leading what is taking place when it comes to the militarization of America's homeland security forces?

Furthermore, the kind of funding and military weaponry that is now in possession of our DHS should be weighed in light of the Constitution, which allows the government "to raise and support Armies, but no Appropriation of Money to that Use shall be for a longer Term than two Years."[24]

The Militarization of America's Civilian Police Departments—and What You Can Do About It

Many of America's police departments have already received weapons that were developed for use on foreign battlefields, not suburbia. In 2014 and 2015, local police departments in America received 1.5 *billion* items designed for the battlefield, at a cost of more than $2 *billion*, courtesy of the US Department of Defense (DoD). Over the past ten years, Tennessee, Arizona, Florida, California, and Texas were leaders in obtaining surplus military gear from the DoD.[25] To put it bluntly, we are designing weapons for war and are now distributing them for potential use on America's streets.

The weapons distributed to local, small-town police departments, county sheriffs, and even junior colleges include, but are not limited to, armored trucks, night-vision goggles, mine-resistant vehicles, helicopters, airplanes, and more. How did this happen—in *America*? We can thank the 1033 Program, created by the 1997 NDAA, which authorized these kinds of transfers of excess military gear to civilian law enforcement. The NDAA gift-giving has no end in sight.

Here is just a very small sampling of how the distribution of military gear adds up across *civilian* law enforcement agencies throughout America:[26]

- 7,091 trucks ($400.9 million)
- 625 mine-resistant vehicles ($421.1 million)
- 471 helicopters ($158.3 million)
- 56 airplanes ($271.5 million)
- 329 armored trucks and cars ($21.3 million)
- 83,122 M16/M14 rifles (5.56mm and 7.62mm) ($31.2 million)
- 8,198 pistols (.38 and .45 caliber) ($491,769)
- 1,385 riot 12-guage shotguns ($137,265)
- 18,299 night-vision sights, sniper scopes, binoculars, goggles, infrared and image magnifiers ($98.5 million)
- 5,518 infrared, articulated, panoramic, and laser telescopes ($5.5 million)
- 866 mine detecting sets, marking kits, and probes ($3.3 million)
- 57 grenade launchers ($41,040)

Some might argue that a 2015 "ban" by the White House against the distribution of military gear to civilian law enforcement agencies ensures that military-grade weaponry will no longer be distributed—but a closer look at the ban reveals otherwise. While it banned .50-caliber firearms, the ban did nothing to affect the more than 84,000 assault weapons the NDAA Program 1033 permits. The White House banned "tracked armored vehicles"—but 87 percent of the 1033 Program vehicles use wheels, not tracks. It also banned "weaponized aircraft"—but none of the aircraft listed in Program 1033 is recorded to have "weapons."[27]

The bottom line is that the majority of military weaponry for civilian law enforcement provided by Program 1033 is still in possession by local law enforcement, not the military personnel and theaters of operation for which it was budgeted, designed, and distributed. The White House ban on the dissemination of military-grade equipment to American civilian law enforcement departments does virtually nothing to prevent the weapons of war from being in their possession—or used against American civilians—in our homeland.

What is even more concerning is that "the federal government does not have a centralized means of tracking exactly how many weapons it gives or sells to police through multiple programs, according to administration officials."[28] And Program 1033 of the 1997 NDAA is just one of seven similar programs that provides money or gear for civilian police departments.[29]

An expert in the militarization of America's civilian police force, Professor Peter Kraska, called the White House actions against Program 1033 "symbolic politics," adding, "This is an attempt by this administration and all the stakeholders to pretend as if they're doing something when everybody knows in their heart of hearts that they are not."[30]

White House Press secretary Josh Earnest's words aligned with

Kraska's: "What we're hopeful that it [the ban] will do, is, it will contribute to the effort to try to de-escalate some of that conflict."[31] But being "hopeful" is not the same as eliminating the 1033 Program altogether. When a law is left on the books, the provisions of the law are still in place until such time that someone challenges its sensibility and even constitutionality. So far, an official challenge has not come.

I have been, and will continue to be, a very strong advocate for local law enforcement having the tools they need to protect our citizens. They need to be equipped and trained to handle *criminals*. At the same time, in our quest for security, we may have created a cloudiness that could encourage an unprecedented use of military-grade weapons against American citizens by nonmilitary personnel on the streets of America. Do we really want such cloudiness to remain? In the name of providing increased security, we may have opened up a Pandora's box, unintentionally making everyone in America more *insecure*.

None of this details the numerous armored personnel carriers the DHS now has and continues to amass, including the twenty-one-foot long, twelve-foot wide (wheel base), ten-foot high Navistar Defense's Mine Resistant Ambush Protected (MRAP) vehicle, which boasts the most advanced body armor technology and has been tested and used in foreign combat.[32] It is built to sustain assaults from mine blasts and improvised explosive devices (IEDs). Is this kind of weapon truly needed here in our homeland? And again, how is it that we are continuing to fund what has become the domestic equivalent of an army while our Constitution still says that while the federal government is permitted to raise and support "Armies," "no Appropriation of Money that Use shall be for a longer Term than two Years"?[33]

Books have been written providing much greater detail about the militarization of our police. My purpose in providing this overview is to help each of us understand that now is not the time for detachment. A significant transformation has already taken place in America, and it will continue if people like you and me allow it.

Don't Throw in the Towel!

After reading this chapter, you may be sitting there in depressed disbelief. I understand. It was incredibly difficult for me to accept the truth, and potential consequences, of what we just covered (and we haven't even scratched the surface). Getting over your initial shock is important as part of the process in moving toward courageous humility. It took me over a year of going through all five stages of grieving[34] over our national condition to get me to the place where I could pull out my laptop, sit down, and bang out this book, with the hope of helping you and others stand and speak with humble courage. If I got to that place, you can get there too.

The bottom line is that you now have a pivotal decision to make. And whatever you decide will have consequences not only for you but also for your children and your children's children.

On the other hand, you may be chomping at the bit, wanting to do something constructive with this news. You may already have started to formulate some ideas of what you can do—ideas that I hope are ethical, legal, and God honoring. We're going to explore how this can be done with even greater resolve and effectiveness in the coming pages.

Keep in mind that courageous humility is demonstrated through *godly* action. It is positive, powerful, and unstoppable as an agent of change. Don't let the bad news leave you crying.

The bottom line is that you now have a pivotal decision to make. And whatever you decide will have consequences not only for you but also for your children and your children's children. It will have consequences for all of America for generations to come. You can put this book down and walk away, pretending you never read it—or you can think deeply about where we now are as a nation and let yourself embrace the need for change. God can use you and me, and many people just like us, as the "horseshoe nails" of humble courage our nation needs.

If there is anything certain, it is that freedom and real, authentic, biblical Christianity need to be revived in America—or perhaps to arise like never before in our history. If that's going to happen, you don't want to sit on the sidelines. You want to get in on the action.

IN A NUTSHELL

COURAGEOUS HUMILITY IN ACTION

Practical Things You Can Ponder and Practice Right Now

- The US government has given our military the authorization to arrest, indefinitely detain, and interrogate US citizens, without trial, legal counsel, or the whereabouts of the arrested individuals being known by anyone but the government. As a Christian living in America, does this concern you? You can humbly demand the revocation of the NDAA. Tell everyone you know about the NDAA. Share what you've read in this book so they are informed. Write your congressperson and encourage others to do the same.

- America's police forces have already been militarized and can continue to be militarized—with weapons created for foreign battlefields. Write your congressperson and humbly demand that this practice stop, immediately, through the enactment of legislation specifically designed to prohibit it.
- History repeats itself for those too indifferent or distracted to ensure it never does. Are you paying attention, taking humble, courageous action that honors God to ensure history is not repeated?

You have a big decision to make in light of what we explored in this chapter, and it will affect far more than your own life and livelihood. Are you okay with America being primed for its own potential Kristallnacht?

You can contact Congress at Congress.gov.

10

How to Handle Racists, #Haters—and Many Folks In Between

One of the hardest things in life is having words in your heart that you can't utter.

—JAMES EARL JONES

I don't have answers for all the possible scenarios you will encounter in our new world disorder. I can, however, offer some insights based on situations I've been in, people I've met, and things that have worked well for me when trying to overcome my own propensity to sit down, shut up, and remain silent. If you're like me, the words of James Earl Jones can apply to many of the people we come across in life. Though he was referring to a speech impediment, many of us can identify with the sentiment. Many of us have a speech impediment of a different kind when we come across a racist or a hater. The same is true when we encounter someone like Lawrence (chapter 4), who has mastered the art of reverse intolerance. We may *want* to say or do something constructive, but sometimes something is blocking us. We just don't know what to do and say when we come across people who are arrogantly self-confident—people who have no problem expressing themselves with a blatant disregard for the feelings of others—people who practice reverse intolerance.

Racists, haters, and the reverse intolerant have mastered the art of intimidation to such a degree that their actions often freeze us into inaction. They know how to stir up the speech impediment in each of us through their arrogance. Courageous humility, however, can warm their frosty effect. It can help put people who are askew in their place—and do so without resorting to as much as a single underhanded tactic. You simply need to prepare yourself.

One of the best ways to prepare to speak up is to think ahead about the kinds of situations and groups of people in which you may find yourself. I've listed some of them here, based on my own experiences. Reflecting on them may help you consider positive ways you can influence people for the best.[1]

The Well-Meaning Misinformed

These are people who don't intentionally oppose the Constitution or Judeo-Christian values, but end up undermining and attacking them by default because they are simply misinformed. Having been confused by revisionist historians, those who downplay and distort the religious roots that helped birth America, they are unable to defend the documents and values upon which America was founded. They don't even see the need for such a defense. You may be one of the people in this crowd. If so, let me encourage you that knowledge is power. If all you do is attentively read through this book, you will be well equipped to educate well-meaning, misinformed people who would be very amicable to the truth—if only someone like you delivered it to them in kind, intelligent ways. (The Suggested Reading List and Resources at the end of this book will help you even further.)

Do your homework. Read. The more knowledge you have about historical facts, the better equipped you will be to deliver them in humble, courageous ways that well-meaning but misinformed people will receive.

The Ill-Meaning Misinformed

Here, we have the people who are intentionally against Christians, against the Constitution, and have an agenda to see it subverted until such time as it can be disregarded and replaced altogether. They work diligently toward that end, doing all they can to convince people to embrace their lies, join the cause, and succeed.

Maybe you picked up this book to learn how to handle these folks, the ill-meaning misinformed. There is not much you can do to convince these people to change their views, but you can focus your attention toward their *audience*, with the hope of keeping them from drinking the Kool-Aid and poisoning their thinking and lifestyles.

I was on the receiving end of this approach many years ago in Chicago, when I was explaining the Bible to people on a subway platform. Two young Mormon men approached me, having heard what I was discussing. As part of their mentoring process, Mormon missionaries are sent out in pairs, with the older, more experienced missionary mentoring the younger. In this instance, the older was quite arrogant, even saying that earlier that morning

God had "told" him that he would "meet a person on the train platform that day who would become a Mormon, travel the world, and preach." He sincerely believed that person to be me. He kept interrupting every time I made a solid point—or tried to—in an effort to keep my words from sinking into the heart and mind of the man he was mentoring.[2] As he persisted, I noticed his young apprentice listening intently. Quickly realizing that it would be futile to talk to the older gentleman, I turned my attention to the younger and pleaded with him about the biblical Jesus. I often wonder, now decades later, where that young man is and what he now believes.

As Jesus warned, don't "cast your pearls before swine" by arguing with people who don't care to listen[3]—but do recognize that not all who hang with the hogs are pigs. Look for teachable people who are being negatively influenced, but who are open to the truth, and direct your comments and actions toward them with humility and respect. You may very well win them over. Remember that weeds grow up with the wheat.[4] Focus your time, efforts, and attention on the wheat, not the weeds, and leave the consequences with God.

The Struggling Disenfranchised

These are people who are struggling with the organized religion, the established church, and traditional views of morality and spirituality. Although not outrightly opposed to God and Christ, they can't seem to get traction in organized religious institutions and are stuck in their journey with God. They are dismayed, disillusioned, or disgruntled over their formal church experience, the moral failures and hypocrisies of spiritual leaders, and are no longer interested in engaging in the circles that produced them. They are spiritual nomads, wandering, in search of meaning, purpose, and some kind of way to fill the God-shaped void within.

You're not alone if you are among the struggling disenfranchised. And I think there are understandable reasons why you're feeling this way. Many of us Christians are responsible, in part, for where you've landed. If I can be honest, I'm embarrassed over many of the interactions I see on social media by people who say they love Jesus in one breath and slam people through their keyboard—or smartphone. Our impatience with people is a reflection of our own wayward hearts toward God, and this is one of the key things that often disqualifies us from being able to gain a credible audience with the struggling, to get to that place where we can humbly speak life into their lives.

I also understand that terrible things have been done in the name of God and of Christ. I understand that many Christians, including me, have lived as hypocrites. But if the strongest leg of someone's argument is the "all Christians are hypocrites" retort, it's a very weak argument. It does nothing to exempt each of us from examining the Lord Jesus Christ, who, at the very least, demonstrated nothing but complete moral consistency; he was nothing close to a hypocrite. If you recognize that others have represented Jesus poorly, why not take the steps necessary to become a great example—someone people can follow as a real, devoted Christian? The failures of others are no excuse for your own refusal to invite Jesus to change your life.

If we're honest, all of us have done terrible things *in our own names*. Pointing out the hypocritical actions of others does not excuse any of us from practicing the integrity we want to see in others. Tossing out baby Jesus with the bathwater of hypocrisy is no excuse for rejecting the Bible, Jesus, Christianity, and Judeo-Christian values. If hypocrisy bothers you, and that is your reason for rejecting the Bible, Jesus, Christianity, and Judeo-Christian values, then make it your ambition to be the world's greatest "anti-hypocrite," the real deal, a person who actually lives by the moral principles you want to see everyone embrace. Don't let the failures of others keep you from your own success.

Each of us needs to rediscover that Jesus Christ, not the church, died for our sins. We need to understand that while man will let us down, the Son of Man, Jesus, never will. We need to understand that the hope and change we seek is only found through Christ and through embracing his teachings found in the Bible.

What many of the struggling disenfranchised need to see is real humility and kindness coming from those of us who say we have a personal relationship with Jesus Christ. Many of us in organized religious circles have become the biggest obstacles to people coming to saving faith in Christ. We need to ask God to forgive us. And we need to change our ways. Have your words been less than humble? Do you tend to miss opportunities to reach out to people who have been turned off, not by Jesus, but by his "followers"? Now would be a good time to stop being a stumbling block in the lives of others.

Maybe you've focused on being bold without realizing the importance of loving actions that should accompany your words. It's often not what we say but how we say it that convinces people of the truth. Are your words, bold and truthful as they may be, merely giving people a headache? Consider Paul's words in 1 Corinthians 13:1: "If I speak in the tongues of men or of angels, but do not have love, I am only a resounding gong or a clanging cymbal."

How we say what we say, not merely what we say, is a crucial aspect of the Christian faith. If you embrace humility and seek love as the first and driving force behind all you say and do—if you really make the well-being of other people your passion—you will find yourself with countless opportunities to speak with humble courage about the issues of the day toward the struggling disenfranchised. This approach is exactly what made Jesus so consistently attractive to the tax collectors, prostitutes, and other sinners. If that approach is found in you, people will flock to you like birds swooping down upon suet[5] on a cold, winter afternoon.

The Reverse Intolerant #Hater

First, let me explain that by using the name #Hater or "hater," I don't mean it to belittle someone's dignity but to describe someone's behaviors. Lawrence, whom we met in chapter 4, is an example of a genuine hater, unaware that he is practicing and promoting the very things against which he rants. These kinds of people openly, confidently reject the millennia-old teachings of the Bible—especially about sex and sexuality—and enjoy expressing their hostilities toward people who believe differently. Often, they also deny the truth that the Declaration of Independence, the Bill of Rights, and the US Constitution, as well as the constitutions of all fifty states, were heavily influenced by Judeo-Christian principles stemming from the Bible. They live in a self-imposed exile from historical fact, and work tirelessly to try and get others to embrace their misgivings and accompanying disgruntlements.

People who practice reverse intolerance aggressively look for ways to change majority thinking and cultural norms. They are against historic, Judeo-Christian practices and the application of the Constitution in keeping with its historical meaning. Don't let them intimidate you. There's a cure for that coming a few pages down the road. It's enough to say right now that your respect for God needs to outweigh your fear of people. That is the secret to courageous humility.

The Modern-Day Pharisee

Maybe you are becoming a hypocrite and legalist, a modern-day Pharisee—and you don't even realize it. No one wakes up in the morning and intelligently decides, "I think I'll be a complete hypocrite today. I think I'll focus on impressing others but neglect my heart for God," but it can happen nonetheless. It's much easier to be a walking contradiction than it is to be a living sacrifice (Rom. 12:1–2).

Believing the Bible is God's Word is not enough to keep you from gradually changing, unknowingly, into a modern-day Pharisee. With the passage of time, your study of the Bible can lead you to legalism rather than liberty, and to possessing a critical, judgmental attitude you don't realize has crept in. You can end up being more like some of Jesus' archenemies, rather than his friends, the disciples.

The words Jesus spoke to the Pharisees in his day about their love for Scripture, while missing him as he stood in their midst, should serve as a warning to any Bible-believer today:

> You study the Scriptures diligently because you think that in them you have eternal life. These are the very Scriptures that testify about me, yet you refuse to come to me to have life. (John 5:39–40)

As a pastor, I can tell you that it is all too easy to become satisfied with the knowledge of God's Word rather than intimacy with the God who keeps his Word. It's too easy to have a "ministry mistress" rather than to have a wholehearted love for God and people, which is the greatest of all pursuits in life (Mark 12:30–31).

If loving God and people is not the result of your reading and study of the Bible and ministry, it's a strong sign that legalistic, hypocritical self-righteousness has taken over. This is one of the reasons why many people are turned off by church (and rightly so). *Pastors and Christian leaders, are we listening?*[6]

The Member of the Nighttime Bible-Reading Society

Remember Lawrence, the master of reverse intolerance in chapter 4? I referred to him as an unintentional member of the Nighttime Bible-Reading Society (NBRS). His beliefs about the Bible—and Jesus—would just as well arise if he were reading the Bible at night, lights off, sunglasses on—with one eye closed. Most people would never expect to make any sense of a book they approached this way, yet many people, like Lawrence, might as well get on with it and officially adopt the NBRS approach to reading the Bible.

In contrast to the modern-day Pharisee, who is very legalistic and self-righteous, someone in the NBRS can be quite liberal and seem very accepting at first. They may even be very pleasant to be around at times, but that does not make his or her misreading of the Bible something more tolerable to God or beneficial to people.

When we read only select portions of the Bible and cut out the parts we don't agree with, we end up missing large, vital portions and recreate God in our own image. As a result, we end up living far below our created potential.

Consider some of the things Jesus said about truth and his relationship to it:

> You will know the truth, and the truth will set you free. (John 8:32)

> Everyone on the side of truth listens to me. (John 18:37)

The surest way to withhold truth from yourself, and from others, is to edit the Bible to your liking. You'll be well on your way toward not only recreating God in your own image but also failing in more ways than we can recount here.

The most unloving, hateful, harmful thing we can do is withhold truth when we know what it is.

If you know someone who is a NBRS member, don't apologize for the truth found in the Bible. Share the truth of God—with humble courage. Remember that the Great Commission is to not merely baptize people but to teach them *all* Jesus' commands:

> Therefore go and make disciples of all nations, baptizing them in the name of the Father and of the Son and of the Holy Spirit, and teaching them to obey *everything* I have commanded you. (Matt. 28:19–20)[7]

When we stand up and speak out about the teachings of the Bible, we don't do people a disservice; we help set them free. The most unloving, hateful, harmful thing we can do to anyone is withhold truth when we know what it is. The most loving thing you can do is tell people the truth, humbly yet courageously, because truth is the exact thing they need, even if they don't yet realize it.

The Wealth-Seeking Worrier

In the parable of the sower (Matt. 13:1–23), Jesus warned against being the kind of person whose life is characterized by the "worries of this life and the deceitfulness of wealth" (v. 22). Such worries and misdirected efforts will do nothing but "choke the word, making it unfruitful." Has God's fruit in your life been choked off because you've been pursuing something other than God?

First Timothy 6:9 says it this way: "Those who want to get rich fall into temptation and a trap and into many foolish and harmful desires that plunge people into ruin and destruction."

Have you become a wealth-seeking worrier? Has the pursuit of money distracted you from pursuing God? It's not possible to stand up and speak out with humble courage, to address the problems of society, if you're not addressing this fundamental distraction if it exists in your own life.

Deal thoroughly and continually with wealth-seeking worrying—and follow God with humble courage. Then you'll be in a good position to help others follow your lead. They will see that your real net worth is found in God, and you'll become contagiously irresistible.

Living with power and courage, instead of weakness and fear, is possible when we deal with the dilemmas and distractions in our own lives. How can you make practical changes in your life right now to help you be a positive factor of influence in our increasingly negative world? Why not put those changes into practice today?

IN A NUTSHELL

COURAGEOUS HUMILITY IN ACTION

Practical Things You Can Ponder and Practice Right Now

- Are you as knowledgeable about American history as you should be? Imagine how reading just a few solid books about the founding of America and our Constitution will help you be able to stand up and speak out. For starters, check out The Heritage Foundation (http://www.heritage.org/) and First Liberty (http://firstliberty.org/).

- Have you become an unintentional hypocrite, a modern-day Pharisee? Check out the appendix, "Ten Signs You May Be Morphing into a Pharisee."
- Are you a member of the Nighttime Bible-Reading Society, reading the Bible selectively, unintentionally recreating God in a new, distorted image as a result?
- Are you distracted, pursuing something else more than God? Are you married to the ministry rather than in love with God? Have you become a "human doing"?

11

Secret Weapons

Hidden in Plain Sight

The best way to keep a prisoner from escaping is to make sure he never knows he's in prison.

—FYODOR DOSTOEVSKY

None are more hopelessly enslaved than those who falsely believe they are free.

—GOETHE

Courage isn't something we're born with; it's something we develop. It's time to throw a party, because this is great news in an age of fear. Courage gives no preferential treatment to color, sex, age, or wealth. It is, therefore, available to everyone. The question is, Where does courage come from, and how can it be cultivated? Without courage we will cower—and cowering always leads to defeat, which leads to enslavement. The cultivation of courage is, therefore, one of the most important things in all of life.

"Everybody wants to save the earth," said P. J. O'Rourke, "nobody wants to help Mom do the dishes."[1] If we want to change the world, we can begin by doing things that are right in front of us, within our reach. We can work on the things that are obvious, within our grasp. One of the most practical, powerful things you can do is change the way you think. This is exceptionally important, because thinking has everything to do with courage. You have the capacity to change how you think, and this means you can become a person of courage—humble courage.

The reason you need to change your thinking is because if you don't, someone else will. It's just a matter of time. In the end, a great deal comes down to who or what wins the battle for your mind. Romans 12:2 confirms this: "Do not conform to the pattern of this world, but be transformed by the renewing of your *mind*. Then you will be able to test and approve what God's will is—his good, pleasing and perfect will."[2] As your mind goes, so goes everything about you, for better or worse. (Did you notice from these verses that clarity over God's will is a by-product of a renewed mind? A renewed mind is also the by-product of not conforming to the crowd, the "pattern of this world.") Your mind is ground zero in the battlefield for courage. If you change the way you think, you can live with power, truth, and love in an age of intolerance and fear. If you don't, you're destined for the exact opposite.

Brainwashing and reprogramming are so much a part of our culture that we don't realize what we often think and do are simply because we've been *told* to think and do, not because something may be true, good, noble, and just. We have lost our ability to think for ourselves. We just think and do because it's what everyone else is thinking and doing, and we keep heading in the same direction—away from objective truth, reason, and God. As we move away from God, we move farther and farther away from all the blessings that accompany him, without realizing we are forfeiting the best quality of life possible, courtesy of life's Designer. We have come to the point where we want God's blessings without God's conditions for the blessings. We are attempting the impossible.[3]

The attack on thinking is nothing new. It just seems that the majority of Americans no longer care to resist. We embrace mediocrity, or worse, for no reason other than that we think an outcome is inevitable. The daily, moment-by-moment bombardment of advertisers, media, pollsters, and politicians—courtesy of our smartphones, tablets, televisions, and computers—has conditioned us to accept things as if they were inescapable facts, when they are often just cleverly delivered *opinions*. This information is purposely packaged to make us cry *uncle*, to accept the lie that resistance is futile. Godly resistance, however, is the very heart and soul of humble courage.[4]

Where are we at this vital time when America is melting down? We're not paying attention to the real world but are allowing ourselves to be distracted by the virtual one. We spend more time on our devices than we do sleeping;[5] we spend more time being told what to think, believe, feel, and accept than we spend thinking for ourselves. If there is any hope for us, for our families, for our houses of worship, and for our nation, we must rebel against being conformed to the pattern of a culture that is racing away from God with celebratory glee.[6] Our rebellion against the culture must go into overdrive, because we have a great deal of catching up to do with God.

Is *Google Syndrome* Crippling Our Thinking?

"Critical thinking," said Michael Bugeja, "can be accelerated multifold by the right technology."[7] Bugeja is director of the Greenlee School of Journalism and Communication at Iowa State University of Science and Technology. However, he said, "The technology distraction level is accelerating to the point where thinking deeply is difficult. We are overwhelmed by a constant barrage of devices and tasks . . . We increasingly suffer from the Google syndrome. People accept what they read and believe what they see online as fact when it is not."[8]

Patricia Greenfield, a UCLA distinguished professor of psychology and director of the Children's Digital Media Center, Los Angeles, believes decreased reading, combined with an increased use of technology, has contributed to our decline in critical thinking. "There is a greater emphasis on real-time media and multitasking rather than focusing on a single thing," as happens when we read.[9]

After scrutinizing more than fifty studies on the impact of technology and multitasking on learning, Greenfield said, "Reading enhances thinking and engages the imagination in a way that visual media such as video games and television do not . . . .[Reading] develops imagination, induction, reflection, and critical thinking, as well as vocabulary."[10]

Visual media has been shown to improve the ways in which we process some information, but "most visual media are real-time media that do not allow time for reflection, analysis, or imagination," she said.[11] The result is that those who are using visual media the most (young children and young adults) are not maximizing their "intellectual potential."[12]

Parents who use smartphones, tablets, television, and video games as pacifiers to placate sulking babies, entertain toddlers, or accommodate demanding teenagers may want to think long and hard before continuing this practice. In the long run, doing so may be hindering our children's ability to develop deep thinking and social skills. We may be perpetuating societal decline by unwittingly transforming our children into nonthinking, compliant imbeciles, trained to go along with what everyone else is thinking and doing.

So what is a parent to do in this busy world where multitasking is esteemed as a supreme parenting skill? You do what parents and guardians did for millennia, before the propagation of electronic devices. We have to stop treating parenting as a hobby, rather than as the tremendous, full-time responsibility it is. Keep in mind, parents and guardians, that you will one day give an account before God for how you raised your child. If you don't pay attention to your child, someone else will.

Parents and guardians, think about this long and hard. Make adjustments to your parenting as needed, because how you parent will be the most impactful factor on your child's emotional and intellectual development, and their ability or inability to live with courage, power, truth, and love.

God hasn't called you to raise a zombie. He's called you to raise a man or woman of God who thinks deeply, engages fully, and walks in the power of the Holy Spirit as an agent of salt and light in an increasingly dark and distasteful world.

Singletasking, Digital Media, and Social Skills

Multitasking, once flaunted as a skill, may actually be a hindrance when it comes to recalling information and facts. A study of college students watching *CNN Headline News* without the news ticker on the lower third of the screen revealed that such students had better recall of what they watched and heard than those who watched with the news ticker. Greenfield, who reviewed the study, said it is just one example of similar research that suggests multitasking hinders our comprehension.[13]

A decrease in real, personal interaction with people, coupled with an increase in the use of digital media, hinders social skills among children, said UCLA scientists. They discovered that eleven- and twelve-year-olds who "fasted" from any exposure to television, smartphones, and digital devices were far better at "reading human emotions" than those from the very same schools who used electronic devices daily.[14] In other words, an increase in the use of electronic gadgetry, coupled with a decrease in face-to-face interactions, hinders our ability to empathize and interact with one another.[15]

Isn't it ironic that our social media age is actually damaging our real, meaningful social interaction? Social media may, after all, be *antisocial* media, keeping us from the kinds of meaningful thinking and interaction that we crave, need, and for which we were designed in order to honor God and make positive contributions to society.

We must regain the art of *singletasking*—the ability to focus on one thing at a time so we may comprehend exactly what we're experiencing, be truly engaged, and respond accordingly. If we want our children to be emotionally healthy, to have increased comprehension, and to think deeply, critically, and productively, we must greatly reign in our own use of smartphones, tablets, television, and video games—but doing so will not be enough. *We must do more.*

Deep, critical thinking that is vital to the exercise of courage (the very thing that determines our ability to rebel against the status quo in healthy, God-honoring ways) must be "revived." (We may soon discover that *revived* is not the most appropriate word if our next generation matures without developing solid critical-thinking skills in the first place.) If we do not (re)gain the ability to think critically, we will not be able to stand up and speak out, because we will not even understand there is great need to resist.

To develop humble courage, we must (re) discover the weapons in the original war on terror—the weapons any one of us can wield, the weapons that have been hiding in plain sight.

To think deeply and develop humble courage, we must

(re) discover the weapons in the original war on terror—the weapons any one of us can wield, *the weapons that have been hiding in plain sight.* These are the weapons necessary to combat our cowering.

Winning the Original War on Terror

In my struggle against the things that terrorize me, I've found three indispensable weapons that have transformed my walk with God, my interactions with people, and, in fact, my entire life. These weapons can do the same for you. They are the Holy Spirit, genuine repentance, and intentionality. These three, when united, make you invincible to cowering. They cannot be overcome by even the most formidable foe.

Each of these weapons has always been available to you, although the daily chatter of life, the things that masquerade as being important, have rendered them hidden in plain sight. It's time you and I release them—to their utmost—in our lives. Once we do this in our personal lives, families, and houses of worship, the revolution of humble courage will eclipse the onslaught of fear. These weapons are the tools you need to execute the turnaround we've all been waiting for in our churches, homes, and businesses, and in our country.

Weapon 1: The Holy Spirit

> For the Spirit God gave us does not make us timid,
> but gives us power, love and self-discipline.
>
> —2 TIMOTHY 1:7

People of every religion pray. Many people meditate. Even Christians are called to meditate, but to do so in fundamentally different ways than every other religion. Christian meditation is based squarely on the Word of God, the Bible. The psalmist wrote, "I meditate on your precepts and consider your ways" (119:15).

Psalm 1:1–2 says:

> *Blessed is the one*
> *who does not walk in step with the wicked*
> *or stand in the way that sinners take*
> *or sit in the company of mockers,*
> *but whose delight is in the law of the Lord,*
> *and who meditates on his law day and night.*

The words in Joshua 1:8 should motivate us to make the Bible the centerpiece of every day:

> Keep this Book of the Law always on your lips; meditate on it day and night, so that you may be careful to do everything written in it. Then you will be prosperous and successful.

The verses above are just a sampling of many in the Bible that demonstrate how God transforms what would otherwise be ordinary lives into extraordinary lives of courage.

But is that all? Is courage simply a by-product of meditating on God's Word? You may be surprised to learn that I don't think it is. It's possible to meditate on God's Word without putting it into practice. Such meditation is really useless self-deception, and many people practice it without realizing it is a waste of wisdom and time. Jesus said, "Blessed rather are those who hear the word of God and *obey* it" (Luke 11:28).[16] James 1:22 says, "Do not merely listen to the word, and so deceive yourselves. *Do what it says.*"[17] Our lives are transformed, and become powerful vessels of the courageous Holy Spirit, when we put the Word of God into practice.

Something happens within us every time we meditate on God's Word with a commitment to do what it says. It happens because to spend time in God's Word is to do something far more—it is to spend time with God himself. When we commit ourselves to putting God's Word into practice, we become filled with the Holy Spirit, and he removes all competition. This is a crucial understanding we have forgotten in the land where Bibles and Bible-teaching ministries abound.

The Holy Spirit is God the Father's not-so-secret secret weapon against intimidation and fear. *He is the Spirit of boldness.* He is the One who knows what to say—in precisely the right way, at the perfectly right time. As you spend time in the Bible, the Holy Spirit will well up within you and spill over into your time apart from the Bible—if you are serious about applying what you read. The words of God, combined with the power of the Holy Spirit, will begin to guide you throughout the day, and you will begin to see fear evaporate over time as boldness for what is right in God's sight takes over.

> The Holy Spirit is, however, a gentleman. He does not force himself upon us, but moves in power when we remove the kinks in the garden hoses of our lives.

Give Way to the Divine Gentleman

The Holy Spirit is the same One who welled up in Peter on the day of pentecost, leading him to preach his rousing sermon that brought three thousand people to the feet of Jesus. He is the same One who filled Peter again in Acts 4:8, when he confronted the leaders of Israel who were still rejecting Jesus Christ. The Holy Spirit is the same One who empowered each and every one of the biblical characters we read about in chapter 3, "Heroes and Underdogs." The

Holy Spirit is the One who will transform you into a person of power, truth, and love so you can stand up and speak out whenever and wherever God wants a messenger.

The Holy Spirit is, however, a gentleman. He does not force himself upon us, but moves in power when we remove the kinks in the garden hoses of our lives. The Holy Spirit fills us up when we empty ourselves of things that are contrary to God. The kinks in our lives, courtesy of sin, affect not only our relationship with God but also our relationships with people, and enslave us when we would otherwise walk in freedom. This is why the next weapon we discuss is vital to the unhindered movement of the Holy Spirit, so that courage, rather than cowering, becomes the increasing characteristic of your life.

Weapon 2: A 180-Degree Lifestyle

Janet and I started the National Week of Repentance™ (WeekofRepentance.com) because we see the need in our own lives, along with the deep need in our nation to repent. We're living in such a distracted nation that a single day is not long enough to think deeply about our lives, assess what's out of whack, and cooperate with God so that he realigns us with his heart, mind, and mission.

No one who truly surrenders to God will ever live to regret it.

One of the key traits of a Christ-follower is the growing ability to hear God—and to immediately adjust life to what he says. If this is not a growing reality in your life, it's a good indication you are not following Jesus Christ. We must remember that no one who truly surrenders to God will ever live to regret it. But there are a great many people who have resisted God and lost time, money, happiness, and much, much more in the eternal scheme of things. Why resist God for even another moment?

In a Word

The word that summarizes the primary characteristic of a genuine Christ-follower is *humility.* A humble person is someone whose lifestyle is marked by continual repentance—turning away from everything contrary to the heart, mind, and will of God and submitting to him fully. Humility and holiness, therefore, are inseparable traveling companions on the same journey toward Christlikeness.

In order to truly follow the Lord Jesus Christ, 180 needs to become your favorite number because of what it reminds you to embrace when it comes to walking with God. A 180-degree lifestyle of repentance is the universal call of Jesus to every single disciple. There are no exceptions. Without a lifestyle of humility, it is not possible to follow Jesus Christ as the Master of your life or to reach your greatest potential. Only a repentant lifestyle, a lifestyle of humility that continually points all of life toward God's glory, can consistently unleash his power. Once you embrace 180-degree living, you begin to become God's catalyst for supernatural transformation everywhere you go. Until you do, you're wasting precious time that could otherwise be energized by the very power and presence of the Almighty.

Today will take its place as a tile in the mosaic of your life. You are either following Christ in growing humility or you are following someone or something else.

Would you like to know a secret? The reason we are seeing so much division and so much hatred toward God and people in the world is because the opposite of humility and a lifestyle of repentance is running rampant in America and around the world. The opposite of humility, of 180-degree living, is pride.

Today will take its place as a tile in the mosaic of your life. You are either following Christ in growing humility or you are following someone or something else. The lie that we often believe is that there is satisfaction apart from God, but the truth is that God is the Author of all satisfaction. To live a surrendered, 180-degree life of humility is to live a life of divine satisfaction. It is to live a lifestyle of repentance. When we compromise our surrender to God, we end up being enslaved to one or more false gods—gods that cannot match the living and true God's mercy, grace, power, and beauty, or the satisfaction that he alone provides.

Silence Speaks

God is often silent when he is preparing to say something big. In other words, the silence of God is the silver platter upon which the golden apple is often set. Never, therefore, belittle the silence of God. The Master, even in silence, speaks.

There was a season when God was silent for four hundred *years.* His silence was between the time of the prophet Malachi and the opening words of Jesus Christ, recorded in Mark's gospel.

It's the way God broke his silence through Jesus that should stop us in our tracks—and move us forward. Jesus' words reveal our need for the transforming touch of God and how fundamentally out of alignment we are without him. His words are simple, but by no means insignificant. They are meant to change everything about us, *from the inside out.*

Here are the words, carefully selected and masterfully delivered by Almighty God himself, when he came on the scene and broke his four hundred years of silence: "'The time has come,' he said. 'The kingdom of God has come near. Repent and believe the good news!'" (Mark 1:15).

The verb tense in the Greek language that Mark used would be better translated into English as "repent and keep repenting" and "believe and keep believing." This magnifies the significance of Jesus' words. A more accurate translation of his words in the English language reads like this: "The time is fulfilled, and the kingdom of God is at hand; repent and keep repenting, believe and keep believing in the gospel." This understanding will release you into a life of power, truth, and love.

Combating "Self" with the Grease of Life

Every follower of Jesus Christ had an initial moment of repentance and belief. There is a first time when a person comes to terms with Jesus being God, Savior, and friend. You may not recall the day and hour (I don't remember mine), but you should at least remember the season when your life warmed to Christ and you took your very first steps in your 180-degree journey. But your first steps were simply the beginning of an entirely new way of life that should become increasingly clear as you continue to pursue Jesus. All of this is made possible through the undeserved favor of God, through a new approach to life characterized by repentance.

The life of a Christ-follower is to be characterized not merely by belief, but by daily and moment-by-moment repentance. In short, we need to turn from the sins of self-glorification and of self-protection, because they are the manifestations of pride. All sin can be categorized into one, or both, of these practices. We tend to gravitate toward our own comfort, convenience, and safety—but the great work of the Holy Spirit is to move us toward living a courageously humble, powerful life, characterized by truth and love that puts God first in all things and in every endeavor. Everything we think, dream, and do is to be marked by the increasing leadership of Jesus Christ and his character that is manifest in our lives as a result.

As John the Baptist said of his cousin Jesus, so should we: "He must become greater; I must become less" (John 3:30). A newfound love for God compels a person who bears the name "Christian" to actually *follow* Jesus Christ. Surrendering fully to God never limits us. It sets us free. It enables us to not only think about living lives of humble courage but to also see such lives become reality.

Who is it that you need to forgive today? Who do you need to seek out and ask for forgiveness? What do you need to stop doing—or start doing—so you can live a surrendered life, marked by the Holy Spirit of fearless courage, flowing with truth and love? Why postpone it any longer?

When things go well with God and people, all of life is wonderfully lubricated and things run smoothly. If you haven't found this to be true, today is the day to take God at his word and surrender to him fully by repenting thoroughly and making repentance your new way of living. Until you do, the kind of abundant life that Jesus promises in John 10:10 will unnecessarily escape you. The abundance Jesus promises (which many people have sadly perverted into a puny promise for financial prosperity) has to do with things far more important than mere money. His abundance encompasses every area of life, beginning with, and centered upon, his glory, not our own accumulation of material possessions.

Repentance is the grease of a life filled with the Holy Spirit, and it is absolutely essential to make it the number one characteristic of your life if you want to be able to stand up and speak out for the glory of God and benefit of your family, your church, and our nation. Without repentance as a lifestyle, you won't reach your full potential with God or people.

Repentance is the grease of a life filled with the Holy Spirit.

Repentance, a daily, moment-by-moment commitment to turn from the ways of the world, our flesh, and the Devil, and to turn toward God, is an invincible weapon in God's arsenal of transformation, making heroes out of cowards. When honest-to-God repentance becomes your way of life, a newfound freedom will begin to spread throughout your life, freedom characterized by power, truth, and love—the traits of humble courage.[18]

Take time every day, throughout the day, to acknowledge and turn from your own sin. Stop focusing on the sins of other people, and start focusing on the removal of the "plank" in your own eye.[19] When you begin to do this daily and moment by moment, you will be in a healthy position to powerfully, lovingly speak into the lives of others to help them do the same. The revolution of humble courage will be underway, and it will all be largely the result of your own repentance and surrender to the Holy Spirit so that Jesus Christ is the all-consuming fire of your life.

Weapon 3: Intentionality

Nothing can compensate for a life lived without intentionality. We need to stop living as if we were wandering generalities and become meaningful specifics with the purpose of taking our nation into new territory where it has never before been, en masse—a nation where humility and courage thrive, side by side, where the power of God is manifest with truth and love. Our nation is long overdue for an army of courageous, humble people who will live intentionally with the all-consuming purpose to advance God's kingdom agenda in every arena of life.

It's time we revisit the two great, inseparable commandments that Jesus says were first among all the 613 Old Testament laws:

> "Love the Lord your God with all your heart and with all your soul and with all your mind and with all your strength." The second is this: "Love your neighbor as yourself." There is no commandment greater than these. (Mark 12:30–31)

These commandments, coupled with the Great Commission, should be the vision of our lives, families, and houses of worship to such an extent that they shape our nation—intentionally. Here, again, is the Great Commission, which must be the mission of everyone who says they are a Christ-*follower*:

> "Go and make disciples of all nations, baptizing them in the name of the Father and of the Son and of the Holy Spirit, and teaching them to obey everything I have commanded you." (Matt. 28:19–20)

We need to stop apologizing for Jesus and his teachings, and for the essential truths that will make our nation greater than it has ever before been. We are not in need of going back but are in dire need of moving forward, of becoming the kind of nation where the power, truths, and love of God are manifest like never before. It's time that the Holy Spirit reigns in you, that you embrace repentance as your new way of life, and that you become intentional in advancing God's kingdom agenda like never before. These are the weapons that will help us live with power, truth, and love in this age of intolerance and fear.

ISIS has shown us what a minority of people can do to instill fear on the majority. Remember, it was an underwhelming *minority* of people, united in a relentless commitment to their cause, that pushed the definitions of marriage and gender identity to where we now are as a nation. A unified LGBTQ community showed us how targeting legislators and legislation, schools and policies, can alter the very fabric of society. Isn't it time that we rise to the highest motivation of all—deep love for God, love for people, and the eternally epic agenda of Jesus Christ? Yes, my friend, I think it's high time we did.

We are in this together, and we must fight, humbly, together. It's time we fight for the greatest King who ever was, and is, and is to come. It's time to become the man or woman of God you were called to be, to put your hands to the plow, as we seek together to build the only kingdom that will last forever.

As we discussed in the beginning of this journey, merely recognizing a problem will do nothing to solve it. What we need today are practical solutions. In the two chapters that follow, we explore practical things you can do in your personal life, family, and house of worship to fight the war of our lifetime and win. And you'll learn how to recruit others to the same. We've already explored many solutions as we've sojourned together—but what you're about to discover will take your entire life to a deeper, higher place of intimacy with God and make a positive impact with people.

IN A NUTSHELL

COURAGEOUS HUMILITY IN ACTION

Practical Things You Can Ponder and Practice Right Now

- If you have friends or family who tend to use electronic gadgets and games, computers, and movies as babysitters, share this chapter with them. They need to know that they are doing a disservice to the well-being of their children. Help them learn the facts and change their parenting before it's too late.
- Look back over the past year or so of your life. Were you characterized as being filled with the Holy Spirit? What did you allow to fill you instead of the Spirit of God? What's keeping you from living a life characterized by courage, power, truth, and love?

- Have you given your life to Jesus Christ as your Savior, as characterized by a 180-degree lifestyle of repentance? Is your life truly marked by growing humility, a lifestyle that is increasingly, entirely surrendered to Jesus Christ?
- Who do you need to forgive, or to ask for forgiveness?
- Are you being intentional about advancing God's will and agenda through *everything* you do, with all your might? What one or two things need to change in your life so that God's agenda becomes your agenda, without compromise?

12

Battle Plan

> The general who wins a battle makes many calculations in his temple ere the battle is fought. The general who loses a battle makes but few calculations beforehand. Thus do many calculations lead to victory, and few calculations to defeat: how much more no calculation at all!
>
> —SUN TZU, *THE ART OF WAR*

If you want to raise good beef, you have to lower yourself to cleaning out the stalls. I learned this growing up on a small farm in the Garden State, New Jersey. Most of the time we were really good about keeping up with Suzie, Molly, and the other cows we named and nurtured, awaiting that bittersweet day when each would go to that big barnyard in the sky and then take up residence in our hungry bellies. Sometimes, though, we put off cleaning out the stalls, until, I'm almost certain, the stench reached to the high heavens, enough to nearly tempt Jesus to return to earth ahead of schedule. Young boys, distracted by the finer things of farm life, don't always do what needs to be done when it needs to be done.

Sometimes the manure would amass until it seemed nearly impossible to find the concrete floor where the cows were making their deposits. But manure wasn't the only thing they'd drop. Mixed with urine, it makes for a goopy mixture not easily forgotten, even decades later. I can still smell the steaming ammonia that ascended into my nostrils on a baking-hot July day—the day I finally remembered that it was my turn to clean out the barn.

Being young enough to be irresponsible (I had waited far too long) and foolish enough to think there was a swift way to make up for lost time, I didn't think much about what I'd wear. The point was to finish *fast* so I could get back to my outdoor classroom: the creek, trees, fields, and pastures where I learned about life not by reading books, but by grasping it with my hands and feeling it between my toes.

A shovel, pitchfork, and a pair of well-made rubber boots are essentials when cleaning a barn, but they are by far not the only necessities. That day I decided to throw those galoshes onto my feet without the comfort of a pair of socks. No time for that—*and no need*; the thick boots would serve as an impenetrable shield, protecting my skin from the straw-mixed, oozing blobs of soaking excrement. There are some things in life that can only be learned by making a mistake, and I was about to make one that truly stunk.

Swinging wide the gate that kept the cows contained, I ventured in. Boots on, shovel in hand, head down in firm resolve, I stepped forward, heading toward the far side of the barn. I determined I would start there, then work my way closer and closer to where I had entered, shoveling one soggy scoop after another. Three steps in, the suction on my boots reached its climax. In my haste to get to the back of the barn and begin cleaning the waste, I lifted my leg, leaving my boot firmly fixed like a helpless soul in quicksand. There, in naked splendor, my foot continued rising, until reaching its peak and hurriedly descending into the thick strata of cow patties.

My attention was now fully engaged: my entire foot submerged, my toes feeling the wet sensation of what had once been in the bowels and kidneys of the animals. When I finally freed my foot, it was a sight that could only be cleaned off with the help of our garden hose, strong soap, and a lot of heavy scrubbing. I slept with my foot on top of my sheets as I lay in bed that night.

If only I had cleaned up that barn when it needed to be cleaned, things wouldn't have been nearly as messy. I learned that day that there is always a high price to pay for putting off what must be done.

We've reached the point in our nation where, thanks to our procrastination, finger-pointing, and our irresponsible stewardship of the divine beauty entrusted to us, we're long past the time when we should have cleaned up our barn. By "divine beauty" I mean the beauty of life, of relationships, and of why we were created in the first place: to love and enjoy God and one another fully. We've allowed ourselves to be amused nearly to the point of death, distracted by pleasures before taking care of the hard work that makes lasting pleasure possible. We've acted like little boys and girls when it's long been time to behave like grown men and women. In so many ways, our behavior has been childish. It's cost us a great deal.

Our microwave approach to solving problems must be exchanged for one more akin to a slow cooker. There is no fast way out of our predicament, yet we must work as quickly as possible to turn things around. We can no longer afford to be detached or to hesitate. Our job is more difficult than it's ever been—than it would have been—if only we had done what we should have been doing all along. We should have been humbling ourselves, pursuing God fully, and loving one another deeply, from the heart.[1] We should not have allowed ourselves to be so preoccupied with changing other people that we forgot to focus on changing ourselves. We should not have allowed ourselves to confuse church growth with genuine discipleship and the pursuit of Christlikeness (we are so adept at caressing speed, size, and numbers). We should have been paying attention to what is taking place in our schools and communities, and yes, even in politics. We should have spent time learning how to communicate and how to resolve conflict instead of pushing it aside for someone else to handle. We should not have allowed ourselves to kick the can of responsibility down the path for future generations to assume the brunt of the burden.

The good news is that slow and steady still win the day. If we will recognize and commit ourselves to a decisive, long-term strategy—if we selflessly consider others better than ourselves and think about future generations (Phil. 2:3)—we can turn things around and even make them better than ever before. Consider the history of the world, even the history of our still-young nation. It was born from hardship, adversity, and conflict. The Allies landing on the beaches of Normandy took great hits but fought relentlessly against impossible odds—and as a result won the day and gave freedom a stay of execution. There is hope for us, today, if we do the hard work, and the *heart* work, of what must be done continually.

The diversity within our nation need not undo us. It could, if we come together in humble courage, even be something God can use to save us.

We're all in this together. The sooner we truly come to accept where we are, the sooner we can get to the hard work of doing what *must* be done. We no longer have a choice. "Failure," as Gene Kranz observed, "is not an option."[2] But in order to win the day, we have to mount up with humble courage and shore up the fundamental cracks in our foundation that have led to our creating, and in some cases inheriting, such a dirty barn.

Time for a Clean Sweep

Right now we need long-term commitment to attentive, steady leadership in our personal lives, our families, our houses of worship, and our nation. Thankfully, it's not the kind of leadership that requires a call to arms by a modern-day George Patton or Douglas MacArthur. The kind of leadership we need can be embodied in the average person—people like you and me—if we will keep things simple, work together, apply ourselves consistently, and encourage one another along the way.

Courageous Humility for Everyone, Everywhere

What follows is a comprehensive battle plan that, if embraced by even a minority of Americans, can get us out of our muck and take us forward. A small, committed, unified minority can move the majority to take action, and don't let anyone tell you otherwise.

1. Reject the *Majority* Myth

Get yourself into the habit of doing what is right in the eyes of God, not what is merely popular, safe, convenient, or comfortable. If you allow those to be your primary motivations in life (as many of us have), you will never be the significant agent of change—the salt and light—God calls you to be.

The King James Version of the Bible is still the world's most popular. In that spirit, I'm going to use a bit of KJV language to make a point you won't soon forget. God spoke through an ass (Num. 22:21–39), used the jawbone of an ass to defeat one thousand men (Judg. 15:15–16), and Jesus hopped on the back of an ass when riding into Jerusalem as Savior and King. God seems to have a special fondness for asses and that's great news for us all (Matt. 21:7–12; Mark 11:7–10; John 12:14). While the world is rapidly changing, God is not changing, nor will he. If God can use an ass, he can use you and me. With a few modern day "asses," God can change the world. But wait a minute, he actually has far more than just a few—and this should inspire you.

What percentage of the population do you think is needed to get the majority of people to embrace a view? Eighty percent? Maybe you think the tipping point is 51 percent? Perhaps you're willing to wager the number is as low as 25 percent? If you think any one of these is the correct answer, you're in for a big surprise. The percentage is far *lower*. One of the biggest misconceptions silencing people who embrace historic, Judeo-Christian values, and those who love the principles upon which America was founded, is that they think society cannot be changed unless an overwhelming majority of the people climb aboard. That assumption is dead wrong. We keep thinking the tide is overwhelmingly against us—and in so doing, we unnecessarily relegate ourselves to the beach, where we sit down and shut up, rather than swimming against the tide to reach our destination. This self-imposed, unsubstantiated belief, which is leading to our defeatist attitude and cowardly behavior, needs to come to an end—today.

Here is a summary of a 2011 study conducted by scientists at Rensselaer Polytechnic Institute that is sure to blow you away—and encourage you to stand with humble courage:

> When just 10 percent of the population holds an unshakable belief, their belief will always be adopted by the majority of the society. The scientists, who are members of the Social Cognitive Networks Academic Research Center (SCNARC) at Rensselaer, used computational and analytical methods to discover the tipping point where a minority belief becomes the majority opinion.

> The finding has implications for the study and influence of societal interactions ranging from the spread of innovations to the movement of political ideals.
>
> "When the number of committed opinion holders is below 10 percent, there is no visible progress in the spread of ideas. It would literally take the amount of time comparable to the age of the universe for this size group to reach the majority," said SCNARC Director Boleslaw Szymanski, the Claire and Roland Schmitt Distinguished Professor at Rensselaer. "Once that number grows above 10 percent, the idea spreads like flame."[3]

The findings of the study are absolutely fascinating—and should encourage you if you embrace Judeo-Christian values and love our Constitution and the principles upon which America was founded. Take heart: there are far more than 10 percent who share your values! Our problem is not that we don't possess these values but that we have allowed "fear pressure," distraction, and other factors we've discussed throughout this book to keep us from standing up and speaking out on the job, in social gatherings, on social media, in school board meetings, and in politics.

If you are a Christian, stop being fearful of speaking the truth, in love, because people need—and even *want*—to hear it. The overwhelming majority of people are on our side. What are we waiting for?

On the Other Hand . . .

The flip side of taking comfort that you are not alone, and that there are far more than 10 percent who share your convictions, is that you must be careful that you don't speak up and stand out only when others are standing with you. If you wait to be in the majority, or even in the tipping point of a minority, it could be a sign you care more about the opinions of people—and your own comfort—than doing what is right in the eyes of God.

Humanly speaking, it is sometimes necessary to stand alone in order to stand for God. History, especially biblical history, proves this. If you are on God's side, you're on the winning side, and that is the only thing that matters. Just as with Daniel, David, Gideon, the apostles, and most of the characters we see in the Bible, there are often times in the lives of real Christ-followers when we *must* do what is right (not necessarily popular at the time), in order to get others to follow our lead. But more than this: even if others do not follow, we must follow God and do what is right, regardless of the consequences.

A weak brand of Christianity, now commonly embraced in many churches and much of America, has convinced many of us that in order to have a witness for Christ, we must comply, be quiet, and turn the other cheek. The culture of Christ has been compromised and obliterated as a result.

A weak brand of Christianity, now commonly embraced in many churches and much of America, has convinced many of us that in order to have a witness for Christ, we must comply, be quiet, and turn the other cheek. The culture of Christ has been compromised and obliterated as a result. The push to be "seeker sensitive" has led us to forget that God is the real Seeker. This is exactly what Satan wants. Consider what Jesus revealed in his conversation with the Samaritan woman at Jacob's well:

> Yet a time is coming and has now come when the true worshipers will worship the Father in the Spirit and in truth, for they are the kind of worshipers the Father seeks. (John 4:23)

Yes, it's good and wise to be sensitive to where people are. Yes, we need to make sure that if people reject Christ, they are truly rejecting *him*, and not because we are demonstrating a lack of compassion or effectiveness in how we are presenting our Lord. Even Paul said, "I have become all things to all people so that by all possible means I might save some" (1 Cor. 9:22). But if in our pursuit to be relevant, relational, and sensitive to people who aren't interested in the things of God we aren't helping people finally make the beautiful plunge of surrendering to Christ, we are being entirely insensitive to the real Seeker: the Lord.

The context of Jesus telling us to "turn to them the other cheek" (Matt. 5:39) is in regard to enduring personal pain from an evil person, not compromising on biblical truth. This is a vital distinction to make. Compromise leads people to deception, puts them into bondage, and robs them of the fullness of following Christ. Biblical men and women of faith, those who exercised humble courage, did what was right in the eyes of God, even if it meant standing by themselves, at God's side. If there is any hope for society, we must regain our footing in this area, where it has been sorely lost.

The Signs

A few signs that we are not walking in humble courage and are more concerned about the opinions of people than we are of the opinions of God ("fear pressure") are when the following kinds of concerns and questions motivate us before we decide to act and do what is right—what really needs to be done:

- "If I stand up and speak out, will people perceive me negatively?"
- "If I do what is right, will it endanger my life, livelihood, comfort, or convenience?"

Those are the questions asked by cowards. It may seem harsh of me to use such a word, but Jesus used it, and we need to heed his warning. Cowardice is not something he took lightly, nor should you and I:

> But the cowardly, the unbelieving, the vile, the murderers, the sexually immoral, those who practice magic arts, the idolaters and all liars—they will be consigned to the fiery lake of burning sulfur. This is the second death. (Rev. 21:8)

Cowardly behavior is just as evil to Jesus as murder, sexual immorality, and the like. If it becomes characteristic in our lives, it's a sign we aren't real followers of Christ. It results in the "second death"—eternal separation from God.

The kinds of questions humbly courageous people ask, which motivate them to act, are very different. They are not concerned with personal safety, security, comfort, or convenience, but with the glory and will of God being honored no matter what. Here are the kinds of questions you and I should be asking one another to help us stand up and speak out with humble courage:

- "If I don't stand up and speak out, will I be disobeying God?"
- "Would my silence in the face of evil be akin to approving it?"
- "What will happen to my children and their children, and to future generations, if I don't do what is right before God?"
- "Does it really matter if others who are not interested in doing what is right and in following God don't follow my lead?"
- "How can I stand up and speak out with humble courage,

> so that when I see Christ face-to-face, he will commend, and not condemn, what I did?"

If you want to be popular with people, you'll never be obedient to God. We must forever resist "fear pressure" and be ever mindful of the reality that our ultimate day of accountability will not be before people but before the Lord Jesus Christ at the "judgment seat" (Rom. 14:10–12; 1 Cor. 4:5; 2 Cor. 5:10). Our cultural priority of putting self above everything is keeping many of us from living lives that reflect the kind of faith we see manifest by people in the pages of the Bible (see chapter 3, "Heroes and Underdogs").

Constantly remind yourself—and your friends, family, and fellow Christ-followers—that if you wait for the majority of people to align themselves with doing what is right, with truly following Jesus Christ, then you take yourself out of the divine equation, disqualifying yourself from being God's agent of change. You must stand up and speak out now, regardless of what others around you are doing. In so doing, you'll be fanning their spiritual flames into fire, so they can also do what is right and honor God.

Here are a few examples to jog your thinking, along with everything else covered in this chapter and the next. (You'll also find great resources designed to help you develop humble courage in all areas of life on Couragematters.com.)

- Pray and stop worrying. Obey God in the little things and you will find that obeying him in the big areas of life will be much easier.
- Write letters, send e-mails, and make phone calls to editors, promoting Judeo-Christian values, letting them know when content from their organization promotes something that undermines the Christian faith or freedom of speech, religion,

or the press. Mobilize your friends and congregation to develop a campaign.

- Write letters, send e-mails, and make phone calls to Congress, letting them know what legislation you approve and oppose. This requires being aware of what Congress is addressing. Congress.gov will provide you with insights. Mobilize your friends and congregation to develop a campaign.
- Write, e-mail, and call your pastor (often) and tell him or her that you want him or her to teach what the Bible says about the issues of the day, current events that are happening locally, nationally, and globally. Your pastor needs to be encouraged regularly. Let your pastor know how much you *appreciate* his or her ministry. Oftentimes pastors hear from people only when they have a grievance. Don't let that be true of you.
- Don't just sit there when people are expressing anti-Christian views. Pray and ask God to give you the words. You'll find that he will. Then, speak them.
- Organize peaceful rallies and contact the media to cover the events. Speak with humility, and if you don't know how to do that, pick up a copy of Dale Carnegie's *How to Win Friends and Influence People*, a timeless classic on how to interact with people in healthy ways.
- Develop your public speaking ability. Pick up *How to Develop Self-Confidence and Influence People by Public Speaking*, by Dale Carnegie. It's a classic that will get you on your way to standing up and speaking out with humble courage.

2. Simplify Your Personal and Family Life

Less Is More. Simple Is Better. If you live in America, there is a good chance you've made life a lot more complex than it needs to be. As we've seen, Americans' time sitting in front of electronic devices is enough to help us realize we need to make some fundamental changes in our lives. We're too busy doing God-knows-what to pay attention to what really matters most. This is true not only as it relates to what is happening in society, but also within our families, our houses of worship, our workplaces, and our communities.

Our busy, complex lives—which we have created for ourselves—add up to a very complex, busy, distracted, detached nation. If we want our country back, it starts with each of us taking back our lives, families, churches, places of employment, and communities. Consider a few questions that can help you cut back and simplify:

- Limit your daily time spent using an electronic device to what is really necessary. Cut it down gradually, over seven days, to see how little you can use it. Take a personal inventory of how much time you spend on your gadgets and you may be surprised how quickly it adds up. On the eighth day, recommit yourself to another seven days of limited use, trying to limit it more each week, to only what is necessary. If you do this for several weeks, one week at a time, you'll reign in "media creep," and start simplifying your digital life for the things that matter far more.
- Do a personal inventory of your life and ask yourself, "Am I really making a distinction between my wants and my needs?" Develop a clear, written vision for your life, with goals that will help you focus on what matters most and keep you from drifting into time-wasters that will sidetrack you. If you haven't done this yet, or you have drifted from your vision, you've set yourself up to be distracted by whatever glittering diversion may come along. Get your life organized around your greatest priorities, and this will help simplify your life tremendously. Maybe it's time to downsize and sell a few things (maybe a lot of things).
- Keep a record of how you spend your money, and see

how you can become a better steward of what God has given you. Stop wasting money that could be spent on better things—like helping people in need, giving to your church, and supporting legislation and candidates who embrace the Constitution and Judeo-Christian values.

- Evaluate if your children really need to attend every social gathering or sporting event, especially if doing so runs the family ragged. If taking your children to these kinds of events keeps you from securing a future of freedom, as we've been discussing throughout this book, wouldn't you be doing a disservice to them, and ultimately to God, by continuing the practice? In many cases children need to do less, and the family needs to be together more, so that the real issues that can plague a family can be prevented from happening in the first place.
- Too many families today live alone together. Homes have different television sets and computers in each room of the house, enabling everyone to live under the same roof without interacting. Set monthly goals for your family time together, including meaningful meals, playing games, doing crafts, and playing sports (not watching them on television), and break down those goals each week, so you are actually spending face time together. And by face time, I'm not talking about using an Apple device. I'm talking about in-person, flesh-and-blood interaction that involves conversation, listening, and enjoying life *together*. This is what brings people together. Just living under the same roof does not count. You need to interact with one another.

How can you better use your time, money, and attention span so that you can direct them to the things that are causing the American meltdown, as we've been exploring throughout this book?

3. Deal Thoroughly with Pornography and Sexual Temptation

Do you have a problem with pornography, or does someone within your family? A pornography addiction will isolate you, harden your heart, destroy your conscience, and open the door to satanic strongholds and serious sexual dysfunction and emotional detachment. And it will significantly cripple not just your walk with God but also with people. *Left unchecked, pornography will destroy you, your family, and your life.* Porn contaminates and complicates all of life. Purify and simplify your life by dealing with porn—thoroughly.

Porn is a major reason why people are not standing up against the filth happening in society—they feel like there is no way out of their hypocrisy and that they are trapped. The good news is that you can end your hypocrisy, get out of the trap, and start standing up and speaking out. Your failures can be the lessons others need to learn from so they are spared from the same addiction. Don't be afraid to share your struggles (and emancipation) with others. Share them so that others can see there is hope for them.

If you have a pornography problem, sign up for accountability software at CovenantEyes.com or with xxxChurch.org (they even have a free "30-Day Porn Free Challenge"). And seek human support and accountability. Deal thoroughly with porn, or porn will deal thoroughly with you.

4. Stop Freaking Out

The world has indeed faced difficult challenges before. Humble courage always won the day, and it will win it again here—*if we practice it.* Aren't you glad the Allies in World War II didn't quit just because the battle was difficult or they were frightened? The same is true for so many of our men and women who fought valiantly for the freedoms that are now being threatened by an entirely new kind of warfare against freedom. It's an all-out war, involving the use of media, the education system, political party platforms, and more—but if we get involved in each of these, along with others, this war can be won. I think too many of us cry *uncle* prematurely.

Yes, the challenge is difficult, but it is not insurmountable. Keep your emotions in check by revisiting historical battles, where people faced impossible odds but still won because they stood up for what was right. The same needs to be true of you and me. Do what's right and leave the consequences to God. Freaking out is the opposite of walking by faith. Romans 10:17 is a great verse to remember, to help you walk by faith, not by fear:

> Faith comes from hearing the message, and the message is heard through the word about Christ.

Remember, to build your faith, lift your Bible. Get God's Word into you so that the life of Christ comes out of you. When you find yourself tempted to cower in fear, pick up your Bible. Go to a quiet, undistracted place, and read it as long as it takes to replace that fear with humble, courageous faith.

5. Don't Use Christ's Return As an Escape Clause

Although I mentioned this earlier, it's worth hitting again—and hard—because so many Christians default toward a divine bail-out approach to life instead of thinking deeply, changing how they live, and genuinely caring about people. I believe in both the Rapture and the literal, bodily return of Christ. You may too. And even if we share different views, we should be focusing on what we agree upon: that Jesus will return. In many circles, however, we have confused fatalism for faith, and irresponsibility with the sovereignty of God to such a degree that we really no longer care about people. We only care about seeing Jesus for ourselves. For this we need to thoroughly repent, change our hearts, and direct our attention to the lost while we still have time.

Lord, save us from thinking that doing what is right is pointless because the time of the end is near! This escape-clause mentality is exactly the diabolical, unproductive attitude many of us need to repent of because it displays a complete lack of love for God and people. It is irresponsible, lazy, and ungodly. For too long we've been using the Rapture and second coming of Christ as excuses for not being the salt and light Jesus calls us to be on earth.

And may I pose a question that I think we have not been asking ourselves, or one another—one that I think we need to begin to ask often? *What if Jesus doesn't come back for a very long time?* Our nearsighted approach to the long-suffering love of obedience is costing us dearly when it comes to standing up and speaking out, reaching as many people as possible for Christ—not because he may be returning tomorrow or taking us away soon, but simply because Jesus is worthy of being loved and followed. It's the identity of Jesus Christ and our love for him that should be our greatest motivators in doing what is right. Things could get far worse before they reach the pinnacle of impurity. The timing and circumstances surrounding Jesus' return should not make a difference in how we are living our lives in the meantime. The only thing that matters is loving God, loving people, and leaving our circumstances up to him.

It could be argued that the apostle Paul thought Christ would most likely return during his lifetime. Many believers throughout history thought the same too. Should speculation about the timing and circumstances of Jesus' return really affect how we live for him today? Not if we are mature in Christ. The mature Christian is motivated by love for Jesus, period. If we study our Bibles and history, we have to admit that we don't know where we are, exactly, in the eschatological (last days) time clock. We could be at the eleventh hour—or we could be at 6:00 p.m., with many more decades, even millennia, to go. Stop focusing on what happens at midnight and pay attention to the time at hand so you can live passionately for God and let him take care of you and the details of life. In the meantime, he never called any of us to sit here and wait to be beamed up.

We know that the Bible teaches Jesus will certainly return. Our focus should be on how we live in the meantime. We should concern ourselves with building the kingdom of God, recruiting others to the same, and living our lives with humble courage. Exchange that "occupy until he returns" ridiculousness for an "advance no matter what" approach. If we all begin to do that, we'll be ready for Christ's return no matter when. But you know what will really change? How we live for him and how we love people—really love them—until we see him face-to-face.

6. #SUSO

Use #SUSO (**S**tand **U**p, **S**peak **O**ut) on social media platforms, to call out people who practice reverse intolerance against historic, Judeo-Christian values. Doing so helps keep them accountable and in check, so that you, who are in the overwhelming majority, don't sit down and shut up. Diplomatically use #SUSO on social media platforms any time you see someone targeting, belittling, and speaking out against patriotic or historic Judeo-Christian values while insisting his or her values get top billing. I can't emphasize strongly enough, however, our need to do this tactfully.

You can always say something kind to make a powerful point, such as "Thank you for sharing, but you're practicing #ReverseIntolerance and that's wrong." You can kindly and briefly make your point, and then end your social media post with #SUSO, so other folks know what you are doing and are also inspired to use #SUSO on social media. This is a great way to rally the #SUSO troops and win small battles on social media that can accumulate, and to get those who practice reverse intolerance to back down. The alternative is that we sit down and shut up—but battles won't be won when we take that approach. Visit CourageMatters.com for examples of how to use #SUSO on social media effectively, and how to stand up and speak out with courageous humility.

When people are being selective in their tolerance, they are being hypocritical whether they realize it or not. Using #SUSO can help keep others accountable to practice the tolerance and love they insist others demonstrate.

7. Remember, It's *Humble* Courage

Be careful you don't practice reverse intolerance by refusing people rights they have as US citizens. We have to be careful that we draw a distinction between biblical values and teachings and the values of the Constitution, which do indeed allow for more than people of Judeo-Christian values to live freely. This may be a hard pill for some of us to swallow, but we need to take a dose of our own medicine and practice what we preach.

So much of today's preaching only tells people what they cannot and should not do, but doesn't help people reach their greatest potential in pursuing God and developing a deep relationship with him. We end up standing for what we're against rather than what we are for.

Yes, avoiding sin is vital if we are going to pursue God, and we need to help people run from sin—but we also need to help one another understand how to run toward the Lord Jesus Christ; to cultivate our hearts; and to be loving, kind, and compassionate toward people who are trapped in sin, deceived, or even outright angry with God or people. This is the way we tolerate people but remain intolerant toward sin. God is the same way. The cross teaches us that God is completely intolerant toward sin. He wants all people, everywhere, to repent. Repentance involves adopting his view of sin, so that we, like him, no longer tolerate it. Repentance moves us toward loving God with increasing fervor, so that we have less interest, time, and energy to do the things that God does not tolerate, and a growing inclination to love him in obedience.

While we should work toward electing legislators and appointing judges who embrace Judeo-Christian values, we need not resort to strong-arm, totalitarian tactics to intimidate people who do not share those views. At the same time we need not apologize for Judeo-Christian values by backing down from our convictions. We can be civil and speak the truth in love in our discussions and debates, demonstrating maturity and a knowledge of the issues and facts (as we discussed in chapter 6, "Speaking Truth with Love").

We can love people without compromising what is right in the sight of God. Who knows? You may even win people over because of your respectful demeanor in this process, and isn't winning people over what it's all about?

It is entirely possible to be tolerant of someone's views that may differ from yours without that tolerance being an endorsement of their behavior. We can fight the good fight without getting into fights that result from a lack of humble courage.

8. Don't Pass the Buck

What would your family, church, and our nation be like if everyone was like you? Are you a model others can follow in good conscience? Don't blame other people for being a problem if you're not making a sincere effort to be the change you want to see in others. Take responsibility for the condition of your life, family, church, and our nation, and stop blaming others.

9. Apologize, Mean It, and Make Amends

Apologizing is a lost art—but it's central to Christian maturity, manners, and healthy relationships. Each of us needs to rediscover the power of an apology. And we all need to make apologizing part of each day, as appropriate. Put what you learn into action, starting today, in every single relationship of your life, and the spiritual awakening we need in our families, houses of worship, and our nation will be under way—and it will have started with little old you at the epicenter.

10. Forgive People . . . Genuinely

Malachy McCourt said, "Resentment is like taking poison and waiting for the other person to die."[4] Do you want to be healthy and happy, and to be a source of health and happiness in the lives of others? Of course you do! Just as there is no such thing as a peanut butter and jelly sandwich without peanut butter, jelly, and bread, there is no gospel without forgiveness, repentance, and reconciliation. If you are a Christ-follower, and you have a hard time forgiving people, you have lost sight of how God, in Christ, has forgiven you.

Forgiveness is not a small thing; it's *everything*.

Like apologizing, genuine forgiveness is also rare these days, and we need to practice it sincerely, perpetually. To err is human, but to forgive is still divine.[5] Forgiveness is not a small thing; it's *everything*. Many psychological and physical illnesses can be traced back to a lack of forgiveness.

Who do you need to forgive—fully? Who do you need to ask to forgive you? Is it possible that you may be the obstacle in someone else's life without realizing it? Humble yourself (see, there's that humility thing again), admit where you may have been wrong, ask for forgiveness, and make things right.

I have found that an amazing thing happens when you get into the practice of forgiving. It becomes easier and easier until you no longer care whether people will think less of you for being honest.

Forgiving others creates positive, forward momentum to do the right thing with people you may have offended by taking responsibility and being an instrument of reconciliation. Develop the great habit of forgiving people and see how God starts showing up in your relationships.

11. Run for Political Office and Support People Who Do

If people who love the Constitution and people of solid Judeo-Christian principles don't run for office and support candidates who do, who is left? Remember that all legislation is an attempt to impose someone's set of morals (values) on others—it's just a matter of whose morals they are and from where they arise. If good people don't run for office, that leaves everyone else to run.

If we want good candidates, then we need to encourage such candidates to run and help them all along. Support them financially. Learn their positions and help articulate them to others. If you are the person who wants to run for office, then learn how to be a better communicator and listener. There is no excuse these days, with all the books, blogs, and resources available, to not improve your communication skills. (Looking for a really obvious hint? Visit CourageMatters.com and download the free *Courage Matters*™ app too.)

12. Remember That Leadership Is About Leading, Not Just Having a Title

It's very easy to think that because God may have placed you in a *position* of leadership (as a pastor, elder, Christian worker, board member, etc.) that you are leading. But leadership is not just about having a position; it's about using your platform to the greatest possible degree. Don't just sit there; stand up and speak out in the platform God has given you, and lead, lead, lead!

13. Spend Time with "Tax Collectors" and "Sinners"

Don't let this become a fuzzy issue with you. Love the sinner; hate the sin—*but make sure you don't reverse the two.* Jesus was noted as being a friend of sinners (Matt. 9:11, 11:19; Luke 7:34). In fact, you were one of them before Christ saved you. He had the reputation of spending time with people who actually needed him; you should too. It's a big mistake that we tend to remove ourselves from the people who need Jesus the most when we should be reaching out to them.

A powerful way you can stand up and speak out is to intentionally seek out people who need God's love the most. Spoiler alert: many such people look hard on the outside but are soft on the inside. Don't let a rough exterior fool or intimidate you. Keep in mind that Jesus wasn't endorsing sinful behavior by hanging with sinners. If you follow his lead, you won't be endorsing sin either.[6] How can lost people find Jesus if the messenger of salvation (you) isn't accessible? They can't. Seek God and ask him to introduce you to sinners so he can save them. You know what? He'll answer that prayer—and you'll be blown away at how God matures you in the process and writes history through *you*.

My father, for instance, was a man whose heart and life seemed so far from God that he would *never* humble himself and repent. In reality, he wasn't that far from God at all. Nine days before he died from a terrible, brief bout with cancer, I had the unforgettable opportunity to lead him to the feet of Jesus. He wept like a baby and accepted Christ as his Savior. But what if I had written him off? It's sobering to think of how selfish I could have been if I had forgotten the fact that Jesus came to save sinners, and sinners get saved when God's people get out of their comfort zones and reach out to them.

Reach out to people, even when they don't look like they are interested. And be relentless, even if you get called names and are uncomfortable. My father even sternly rebuked me a short time before he broke down and repented, telling me I pushed Jesus on him too much. But I knew the eternity he would face without Christ, and God got me past my insecurities so I could focus on Dad's eternal security. I think it's our fear of people, once again, that keeps us from standing up and speaking out to the lost. Don't let that fear immobilize you and rob you of the joy of God using you to set sinners free!

I hope someday to share the story of Dad's salvation in a book demonstrating that *no one is beyond reach.* It's often the people we think are farthest from God who are, in the end, nearest. They are often the low-hanging fruit, the easiest to pick. Don't write people off who you think aren't interested in God—even if they say they aren't, as my father did, vehemently, right up to an hour before he wept like a baby, asked God to forgive him, and accepted Christ. Put your fears and misconceptions about people aside, and reach out to them—often.

14. Rely Upon the Holy Spirit

The Holy Spirit is God's not-so-secret weapon against hatred and opposition to the plan of God and person of Christ. Remember the story of the man I encountered in Speakers' Corner? That interaction was courtesy of the Holy Spirit, who gave me courage and capability when it would have been easier to duck, run, and eat lunch. When the Spirit leads you, you'll please God—and the people you should please. Those you don't please by following God are not people who should concern you.

If you're not a Christian, you can become one right now by acknowledging you've sinned against God, deserve to be eternally separated from him, and want to be forgiven. You need to acknowledge that Jesus Christ died on the cross for the forgiveness of your sins, ask him to be the Lord of your life, and believe that God raised him from the dead. Acknowledge that Jesus is God, that he rose again, demonstrating that God the Father approved of his sacrifice for your forgiveness. Understand, too, that God has plans for you now. He wants you to begin to walk with him now and to begin standing up and speaking out. Accept what Christ did on the cross for you, and surrender your life to him from this point forward. Janet and I would love to know if you made that decision. You can let us know by e-mailing us at CourageMatters.com.

If you are a Christian, but haven't been walking with God, now is a great time to surrender to him anew. He is not just the God of a second chance, but of the third, fourth, and fifth too. He is the God of infinite forgiveness when repentance is sincere. Why not pause in your reading and realign yourself with God right now? After all, it would be ironic to try and stand up and speak out toward others if you were the one who was opposing God by not walking with him, don't you think? If you rededicate your life to Christ as a result of reading this, Janet and I would love to hear from you too. You can contact us through CourageMatters.com.

15. Don't Let Your Distaste for Church Make You Bland Toward Jesus

It's been said that if you find the perfect church and join it, you'll ruin it. Be the Christian you want others to be. Don't make excuses. If the journey of one thousand miles begins with a step, then the revival of one thousand fires begins with a single match. Ask God to make you that match, and he may even transform your entire church community into what you dream about. More important, God may even use you to help shape the kind of church *he* envisions, which, after all, is far more important than the one you dream about.

16. Call, Write, E-mail

On a quarterly or monthly basis, telephone, e-mail, and write your congressperson and senators, humbly reminding them of the importance of following our Constitution; respecting our national history; and honoring our biblical, historic foundations. Organize a group of people (perhaps at your church) and help one another remain accountable for doing this. Remember, if good people detach themselves from the political process, the only people who will be left are those who are not so good, and who will encourage and pass legislation accordingly.

17. Keep Media Accountable

Get involved in the media. Consider a career in journalism or encourage your children to explore that option. When you see or hear distasteful programming, or read something distastefully written, let the station manager or publisher know about it through a letter, e-mail, or phone call. Don't do it just once in a while. In order to stand up and speak out effectively, we need to get into the ongoing practice of communicating every time we see something distasteful, especially when it demonstrates reverse intolerance; distorts history; or promotes hatred, intolerance, or ridicule toward Judeo-Christian values or the people who possess them.

18. Encourage Your Children to Make Influential Career Choices

Look for ways to encourage your children to use their gifts and talents in a career that needs to be transformed by God's power, truth, and love. Yes, every career needs this infusion, but there are some careers that especially need it these days. Whoever controls the media has tremendous power. They have the ability and the resources not only to report news but to shape it so that public opinion is influenced. Legislators, judges, lawyers, and a host of other professions have tremendous influence in how society will be shaped. Encourage your children to use their education to influence people with God's power, truth, and love.

19. Contact Your School Board and Diplomatically Participate in Meetings

Whether you have children or not, your local school board, along with the superintendent and principal, should know you by name because you reach out to them regularly. If you are a pastor, the same is true for you. But don't harass them. Remember the importance of true humility. The local schools should know you are in the neighborhood, encouraging them to do what is right. Don't become known as the person they hear from only when there is a problem. Let them know you are praying for them—and that you will stand with them when they protect Judeo-Christian values and will stand up and speak out with loving resolve if and when they don't.

20. Replicate Yourself

Introduce others to what you've learned in this book, and help them put what you've learned into practice. You have enough material in this book and on CourageMatters.com to spark a humble revolution. Let that revolution begin!

There's enough in this chapter alone, if resolutely applied by just 10 percent of America, that will positively change our entire culture. Living with courageous humility is one of the most practical things you and I can do. It's not complicated at all. It simply requires a desire and the execution of a winning battle plan.

In the final chapter of this epic journey we've begun, we'll explore the power of the "sleeping giant"—the American church—and how, if awakened, it can change the course of our nation for God's good and the benefit of everyone. The myth of separation of church and state has crippled many churches from standing up and speaking out in ways that have always been at our disposal but that we foolishly surrendered. It's time for the sleeping giant to awaken.

IN A NUTSHELL

COURAGEOUS HUMILITY IN ACTION

Practical Things You Can Ponder and Practice Right Now

- Reject the "Majority Myth." There are already more than enough people who embrace historic, Judeo-Christian values to positively turn things around.
- Take responsibility for your own life and actions, and recruit people to practice the things you've learned in this book.
- What are you waiting for? This chapter lays out a practical, powerful battle plan for living with humble courage characterized by the power, truth, and love for God. Don't complicate things. Execute the battle plan, and help others do the same.

13

Awakening the Sleeping Giant

Cultivating a Courageous, Humble Church

> You have forsaken the love you had at
> first. Consider how far you have fallen!
> Repent and do the things you did at first.
> If you do not repent, I will come to you and
> remove your lampstand from its place.
>
> —REVELATION 2:4–5

For the longest time, the church in America has largely confused education with application. Nowhere is this more evident than in how we approach our reading, studying, preaching, and teaching of the Bible. We think that doing so, in itself, brings change. For many years we made the mistake of thinking discipleship was about knowledge, when all along it's been about Christlike courage, humility, truth, and love. This mistake has made many American churches very weak. It is the application of God's Word that transforms Christians and churches into being strong, powerful factors of influence in society.

Discipleship is not merely about Bible knowledge. It's about developing leaders who have Christlike character and methodology. In light of this, I'd like to present a few ideas on how you can be a catalyst for positive change in your own church. The first thing you can do is stop sitting on the sidelines waiting for other people to be the change that can start with you.

1. Make Seeking and Surrendering to God Your Number One Life Priority

Fast and pray until the presence and movement of God becomes the norm in your life and family. Don't settle for doing this alone. Get your family and church to begin seeking God with you. America is long overdue for a mighty spiritual awakening of historic proportions. In fact, we need multiple awakenings, let alone the return of Christ. We've tried a lot of things in our churches, and we want the power of God to move and shake us, and the world—but we have not yet really begun to do what God says his people must do whenever facing insurmountable odds: fast, pray, and repent.

Remember that group of Christian leaders in chapter 1 who misunderstood 2 Chronicles 7:14? The truth is that the majority of us Christians misunderstand it too. When God wants to move and change culture, he begins by moving and changing his people—and it all begins with humility and repentance. True hope and change come courtesy of Jesus Christ, when his people get serious enough to turn from their own sins. When that happens, the spiritual awkening is on, and people will follow our lead.

One of the things that excites me is that the November 2016 National Week of Repentance™ was the first time in US history where a simultaneous, nationwide, *week-long movement of repentance* took place in all fifty states (plus Washington, DC, and

Puerto Rico)—without anyone having to converge in a single location. It marked the first time that technology was used to unite people across America for an entire week under the banner of Jesus Christ—not to ask for spiritual awakening to start "out there," but to ask God to start the spiritual awakening we need one person at a time, beginning with each of us. Taking place the week before the presidential election, the movement even attracted participants from China, Grenada, Canada, the Solomon Islands, Germany, Switzerland, Africa, and more.

Sign up to participate in upcoming weeks of repentance, and get resources to help your family and church develop a plan of fasting and prayer by visiting www.WeekofRepentance.com.

If you are a pastor, take a serious inventory of your life, repent as necessary, and call your people to do the same. If you are not a pastor, encourage your pastor to call for humility, fasting, and prayer, and make sure he or she knows that you have his or her back, and you won't try to undermine him or her. Be humble, not harassing. Don't be bossy; be a blessing. Don't relent until God has complete control of your life, your family, and your church and its ministries. Ask God to start with you, and get everyone you know to start calling out to God to do the same with them.

Remember through it all that you are not seeking God to change other people, but to change *yourself*. If and when you can get even a minority of people in your house of worship to do this and remain faithful, you will see unprecedented spiritual breakthroughs that pave the way for everything else you are going to read in this chapter.

The suggestions that follow for houses of worship will be much easier if fasting and repentant prayer become part of the spiritual fabric in your church. Fasting and *repentant* prayer (distinct from intercessory prayer) become like a hot knife through butter, an unstoppable spiritual factor of influence that the flesh and the Devil cannot overcome. Study the Bible about fasting and prayer, and you will see for yourself. Remember, the Bible is not a book of exceptions but of examples.

2. Schedule a Courageous Church™ conference, watch our live streams, and sign up for news and events at CourageMatters.com.

Download the free *Courage Matters*™ app. Our resources and events will help you and the people you know develop courageous humility and live with power, truth, and love. They'll enable you to stand up and speak out with great effect, and will also show you how to teach others to do the same.

3. Remember Babel . . . and Stop Babbling

Remember how God responded to the people who built a tower to make a name for themselves?

> If as one people speaking the same language they have begun to do this, then nothing they plan to do will be impossible for them. (Gen. 11:6)

If that is God's testimony about sinful people who were full of themselves, then what might be accomplished by a group of people filled with the Spirit, unified for the glory of Jesus Christ, to see his will done and his kingdom advanced on earth? It's high time God's people put aside their differences and focus on who and what we have in common. Until such time, we're wasting time, and things are only going to get worse.

It is amazing what can be done when we only care that God gets the credit.

We have bigger fish to fry than the sardines we are allowing ourselves to nibble upon through our divisions and personal kingdom building. It's time to make sure that our churches are not engaging in "spiritual franchising" (using the name and reputation of Jesus to build our own kingdoms). It's time to revisit our purpose and make sure we're about it: to build the only kingdom that will endure forever—the kingdom of God.

4. Confront the Spirit of Control in Your Life and in Others

The only spirit that is perhaps as prevalent in houses of worship as the Holy Spirit (and sometimes even more so), is *the spirit of control.* Church leaders must deal with the controlling people, or the controlling people will destroy the church by keeping it from its unleashed potential. Church leaders need to humbly, courageously confront controlling people and ask them to step down from their positions of leadership—or lovingly remove them whenever necessary.

It is not harsh to do this unless it is done harshly. Not to deal with the control freaks is to treat the Holy Spirit harshly. I have found him to be a gentleman, as is Jesus. Consider Revelation 3:20, where Jesus is standing at the door of his church, waiting to be invited in. This same Jesus, found in John 20:19 and 20:26, made his way into rooms where the doors were locked. Clearly, a locked door is no obstacle for the Lord. He has the capability to let himself in—but he most definitely prefers to be the invited guest. The spirit of control, whether intentional or not, is what keeps Christ out of his own church.

As when we allow ourselves to be divided, what's at stake when control is not confronted is the unhindered movement of God—which should be the objective of every church and every family. Leadership must arise to remove the controlling corks so the Spirit of God will flow. Don't waste your time allowing or enabling people who should not be in ministry or leadership positions to remain. The life of your church actually depends upon it—and as our churches go, so goes society.

5. Encourage Your Church Leadership to Preach and Teach About Morals and What the Bible Says About the Issues of the Day

The divorce between what is happening in America and what is being preached in the pulpit needs to be resolved and reconciled, and you can help. In many instances pastors are the biggest proponents of separation of church and state. We pastors should apologize to God for being so, and begin to do what we have not, with humble courage. If you let your pastor know that you want to know what the Bible says about the issues we face, there is a higher chance you may begin to hear it. This, in turn, will help all the people in your church know how to walk with God in light of current events.

What many people don't know is that most of the colonial charters, state constitutions, and other important documents of our colonies and states had, or still have, overt statements about God, Jesus Christ, and the Bible. In fact, all fifty state constitutions of the United States clearly thank God for his goodness. It is a complete ignorance of American history—or a blatant attempt to revise it—to suggest otherwise. To see for yourself, here are just a few websites you can visit to read what they say:

- http://www.cnsnews.com/commentary/j-matt-barber/all-50-state-constitutions-explicitly-thank-god-his-benevolence
- http://www.constitution.org/cons/early_state_cons.htm
- http://www.independentamericanparty.org/2014/06/declarations-of-christian-faith-in-americas-colonial-charters-state-constitutions-etc/
- http://www.wordservice.org/State%20Constitutions/usa1000.htm

6. Don't Swallow the Separation of Church from State Argument, Because It Is Not at All Based on Historical Fact

While it is not correct to say that America was a Christian nation, America was *heavily influenced* by the Bible and by Judeo-Christian values.

A church is weak and irrelevant when it does not bring the Bible to bear on the issues of the day. A church may have high-energy music, an engaging children's program, and many other characteristics, but if its leaders are not teaching the people how to apply the Bible to current events, it does not understand a major reason why the Bible was written. It is the guide for addressing every issue of life—especially current events. If we don't examine what the Bible says about issues and events, we'll not just have more of the same we've been experiencing—we'll have more of it, and worse.

What about the fear of your church losing its nonprofit status? The Johnson Amendment, passed in 1954, says that a church may have nonprofit status, with the tax benefits therein, when it "does not participate in, or intervene in (including the publishing or distributing of statements), any political campaign on behalf of (or in opposition to) any candidate for public office."[1] But the amendment does not prohibit church or ministry leaders from educating their people about the issues and bringing the Bible to bear on them—church and ministry leaders are not in any way prohibited by law from doing so. The only thing a church or religious nonprofit cannot do, under the current law, is endorse a particular candidate or piece of legislation—*as an organization*. A pastor or ministry leader, however, may certainly express his or her personal opinion on a candidate or piece of legislation, and may educate people about the issues of the candidates and/or legislation for the purpose of helping others make up their minds and vote as they wish.

You certainly may present members of your congregation who may be running for office and inform your people of their positions, encouraging your congregation to vote for the candidates who best represent Christian values and character.

You can also do much, much more! For more detailed information on what church and ministry leaders can do (you will be surprised at your freedom that you may not be exercising), contact:

First Liberty Institute
2001 West Plano Parkway, Suite 1600
Plano, TX 75075
Phone: (972) 941-4444
Media: (972) 941-4453
http://firstliberty.org/

7. Develop a Ministry in Your Church That Educates and Informs

Meet monthly to organize efforts to write letters to Congress, media outlets, and so on, and educate the pastors and church leaders so they can inform the congregation of current national and world events.

8. Don't Misapply Romans 13:1–7 or 1 Peter 2:13–17

Romans 13:1–7 and 1 Peter 2:13–17 need to be interpreted by other scriptures, such as Acts 5:29. One of the common arguments I hear from well-meaning but misinformed Christians is that we are supposed to obey and submit to leaders because the Bible says so. It does—but not when leaders create policies and lead in ways that fly in the face of God's agenda.

Article II, Section I of the Constitution requires that the president of the United States take the following oath upon assuming office:

> I do solemnly swear (or affirm) that I will faithfully execute the Office of President of the United States, and will to the best of my Ability, preserve, protect and defend the Constitution of the United States.[2]

A similar oath of office is required for other major elected and appointed officials. The success of a public official must be measured by his or her support of the Constitution. For Christians, it must go further. Officials should be screened in terms of how their policies support or obstruct obedience to the teachings of the Bible.

Success in every other aspect of service for a public official will not compensate for failure in unwavering allegiance to the Constitution and support of historic biblical values. No amount of charisma should be allowed to deceive us into accepting a candidate for president or tolerating a sitting president—or any other public official—who is not passionate about preserving, protecting, and defending the Constitution of the United States and upholding historic, biblical values. (Remember, it is charisma that will dupe many into following the Antichrist, while all along he will be acting with diabolical intent and power.)

What If?

What if a president (or any other elected or appointed official) were to act in ways that contradicted or undermined the Constitution he or she swore, on oath, to "preserve, protect and defend"? That would make him or her, by definition, an enemy of the state, a walking contradiction of what he or she swore to do. Such behavior could be an outright, or subtle, act of treason. What, then, of the citizens who find themselves under such leadership? Are we not to take the law of the land seriously, holding all leaders accountable to it? Of course we are. American Christians are called to preserve, protect, and defend historic, biblical Christianity, and (as a matter of abiding by the law) the Constitution. If a leader violates either, we are called by God to resist with humble, resolute courage, to turn things around, not blindly comply and fall back on out of context misinterpretations of Romans 13:1–7 and 1 Peter 2:13–17.

What could happen to America if the Constitution is ignored, belittled, or undermined by the passage of laws that contradict it? Without humble courage to resist tyranny, a war could be won from within, with certainty, by a public official willing to pursue a coy, covert strategy.

If God required our blind allegiance to leaders, regardless of their conduct, we would not be able to celebrate Acts 5:29, which says, "Peter and the other apostles replied: 'We must obey God rather than human beings!'" We are living in an age of growing intolerance toward Judeo-Christian values—and toward Christians and Jews—and it all stems from a root of growing intolerance toward *God himself*.

We need to understand that no law, legislator, policy, or court is above the law and court of God. As citizens of heaven, our first allegiance is to the King and his kingdom. Familiarize yourself with the law of God, the Bible, so that when increased times of testing come, you will know what God's opinion is on the matter, and can stand up and speak out in its defense, when needed.

9. Reject the "You Can't Legislate Morality" Myth

We discussed in chapter 5 the idea that "you can't legislate morality." While this statement sounds wise on the surface, it's actually complete nonsense. All legislation is an attempt to impose somebody's morality on everyone—it is simply a matter of whose morality will be imposed. When you know the morality that God promotes in the Bible, you can hold your head high, in humble courage, and take a stand for what others will surely seek to knock down. In fact, if you are a Christ-follower, you have an obligation—and supernatural enablement courtesy of the Holy Spirit—to do so. Power, truth, and love are yours to dispense, for the glory of God. Dispense it.

10. Remember: History Repeats Itself—If We Allow It

You absolutely *can* speak with tact and grace while you firmly, unapologetically teach, exhort, and educate your people. Remember that when Nazi Germany was being transformed, many pastors and Christian leaders did nothing, when all along they knew they should have been speaking and acting. Those who are not familiar with history are destined to repeat it.

IN A NUTSHELL

COURAGEOUS HUMILITY IN ACTION

Practical Things You Can Ponder and Practice Right Now

- Max Depree said, "The first responsibility of a leader is to define reality." The reality is that churches and religious leaders have allowed themselves to be marginalized when, instead, they should be leading the field. Today we have it backward from what it should be. Our spiritual leaders should be our moral leaders, helping people in every walk of life understand the times, and how to live with humble courage.
- Einstein said that "insanity is doing the same thing over and over again and expecting different results." If we keep doing what we've been doing, we'll keep getting what we've been getting. Is it time your house of worship made some fundamental changes in the ways you are approaching ministry and addressing national and local events?
- If you are a church leader, are you being intentional about developing a humble, courageous church? Why not do all you can to ensure your church is characterized by courageous humility?
- You don't have to wait for other churches to rise up before your church can start. Who knows? What happens in your church may inspire other church leaders and

churches to follow suit. Remember that leadership is influence.

Are you too busy to pray, seek God, and listen to him? How can you lead others effectively if you're not following the Leader?

For resources on how to cultivate a courageous, humble church, visit CourageMatters.com.

Conclusion

Hopefully, this journey we've taken together has cleared your head a bit, diminished fear, and provided hope. I've done my best to give you practical ways to develop humble courage so that you can stand up and speak out with power, truth, and love in an age when intolerance and fear are running amuck.

It's my prayer and deepest desire to see you, your family, your church, your place of business, and your neighborhood become everything God envisions at this vital time in history. I hope this book has helped you, and that you'll share it with others to help them too.

Love God. Hate sin. Have fun. And do take a moment to drop Janet, our boys, and me, a line at CourageMatters.com or on social media. Lord knows we can use your encouragement!

—Michael Anthony

Acknowledgments

My God and Savior, Jesus Christ: You demonstrate everything there is to know about courageous humility. Thank you for your patient love and forgiveness, and for never giving up on me.

My mother, Pearl: Her gift with words instilled in me a love for language at an early age. I always enjoyed watching her type away on her IBM Selectric typewriter (100 wpm!), seeing her make notes in shorthand, and learning from her skillful ability to craft a well-written letter. I miss her, and she is as much a part of this book as am I.

Dave Nace: Your demonstration of humble courage in and outside the classroom is exactly what led me to the feet of Jesus. My struggles with calculus as a high school senior, I suppose, had a bigger purpose in the eternal saga. Thank you for standing up and speaking out when I truly needed to hear the truth.

Paul Rinaldi: Thank you for being such a great fourth-grade teacher, and for inspiring me with that unforgettable writing assignment you gave our class at Franklin Township Elementary School. See what you started?

Dean, Joyce, Mearl, and Gloria Gross: Thank you so very

much for the use of your cabin to hammer out the first draft of this book. Your kindness made this book, and all that happens because of it, possible.

Justin Butterfield, Senior Counsel and Director of Research and Education at First Liberty Institute (www.FirstLiberty.org): Your kindness, expertise, and servant spirit contributed significantly to this book. You were exemplary in every way. Thank you!

Grace Fellowship of York, PA (GraceYork.com): It's one of the greatest honors of my life to love and serve such a fine flock! Thank you for the privilege of being your shepherd, friend, and brother in Christ.

Lisa Jackson, Alive Literary Agency: You are truly a Spirit-led gift from God. Janet and I thank God that you saw something of interest in us, took the risk, and reached out. Wow.

Webster Younce and my friends at Thomas Nelson: I couldn't have asked for a better team! I greatly appreciate your patience, grace, expertise, and wisdom, and I hope we have many fruitful years of productivity ahead. You have been fantastic to work with!

Lonnie Hall: God gave you a vision, and you held fast to it. I'm proud to have you as my friend.

Appendix

Ten Signs You May Be Morphing into a Pharisee

Meanwhile, when a crowd of many thousands had gathered, so that they were trampling on one another, Jesus began to speak first to his disciples, saying: "Be on your guard against the yeast of the Pharisees, which is hypocrisy."

—LUKE 12:1

Are you turning into a person you never thought you'd become? It's possible to start off on the right path but gravitate toward an approach to spiritual "growth" that will leave you dry, empty, and wondering how you got there in the first place.

There were six thousand Pharisees in Jesus' day, and most of them were his archenemies. Today there are millions of "Pharisees." Beware the ten warning signs that you may be morphing into one. But note: the first five signs will probably surprise you because they are actually good things. They are provided to show how much the average Christian already has in common with a Pharisee. The second five are not good at all and are traits that each of us can, if we are not careful, adopt over time. You may have more in common with a Pharisee than you realize.

The Good Things You May Have in Common with a Pharisee:

1. You believe people are immortal and will spend eternity either in or apart from the presence of God. The Pharisees believed this.
2. You prioritize the Scriptures, memorize them, and meditate on them. The Pharisees had the equivalent of a PhD in the Old Testament, yet the hearts of most of them were far from God.
3. You are a firm believer in the sovereignty of God. So were the Pharisees.
4. You believe in angels and the spirit world. So did the Pharisees.
5. You are politically neutral, supporting candidates who embrace and champion values based on God's Word. The Pharisees were the same and did exactly this.

The Pharisees of Jesus' day believed and/or practiced all of the above. These are good things, but they do not guarantee a growing love for God and people. Resting in them alone, therefore, merely puts you on the same page as a Pharisee. Many Christians are comfortable simply embracing these five things, as if, by themselves, they are reflections of love for God. They aren't.

The Bad Things You May Have in Common with a Pharisee:

1. You love the Word of God, the Bible, but you have fallen out of love with the God of the Bible. The chief end of all Bible reading, Bible meditation, and Bible

memorization, is to know, love, enjoy, and follow God. The typical Pharisee had all 613 Old Testament laws memorized, along with so much more, yet missed Jesus when he was right in front of them. They did not understand that the purpose of the Scriptures was, and is, to create spiritual practicality in loving God and people. This is the chief aim of man and the purpose of God's Word.

The Pharisees loved the Scriptures, but they didn't love God and they didn't love people. If you don't have, as a burning passion of your life, a growing love for God and people (both), you are on your way to becoming a Pharisee.

2. You have forgotten that the most important aspect of your spiritual journey and growth is inner purity. Spiritually "good" behavior comes from the inside-out. The Pharisees in Jesus' day thought a person was good because of what that person did and did not do. Jesus, and the Bible, teach us that good behavior is the by-product of inner purity, which God alone can create in a person when he or she repents and embraces a lifestyle of repentance.

   If you neglect inner purity, the starting and ending place of true spiritual maturity, you are on your way to becoming a modern Pharisee.

3. You are impressed with, and even seek, the praise of people. This is spiritual pride. The Pharisees loved the praise of people and having the best seats in the marketplace. They loved to be noticed. It's easy in our social-media–crazed society to start slipping down the slope of liking, even pursuing, human attention. The only attention you need—and will want—if you are growing in your relationship with God is to know God's opinion of you.

   Watch out for spiritual pride. It's deceptive, and it wants to master your life. It will, if you are not careful. You must continually renounce it, or you will be on your way to becoming a Pharisee.

4. You think righteousness can come from anything apart from personal faith in Jesus as Savior, Master, and God. It can't. If it could, Christ died for nothing. In Luke 11:37 and following, a Pharisee invited Jesus to his home for dinner. Jesus went and reclined at the table with him and other Pharisees and scribes (Old Testament "lawyers"). Jesus was right in front of them. Salvation was right at their table. And they missed him! Why? Because the Pharisees thought they could be saved by observing the Law. But Romans 3:20 teaches that is impossible: "For by works of the law no human being will be justified in his [God's] sight" (ESV).

So what was the purpose of the Law? Romans 3:20 teaches that "through the law comes knowledge of sin" (ESV). The Pharisees thought observing the dos and don'ts of the Old Testament would save them. Actually, the purpose of those dos and don'ts was to teach that God's standard is perfection and can't be attained without divine help. In other words, God wanted us to see that we fall short, that "all have sinned and fall short of the glory of God" (Rom. 3:23 ESV). Then, and only then, can we realize that we need God to rescue us. Hence, the Savior, Jesus.

If you think you can be saved by being a good person, you miss the whole point. No one is good enough, nor can anyone be good enough. If you're trying to be good and attain God's forgiveness and personal purity by obeying the Bible without doing so out of love for God, you miss the whole point and are on your way to becoming a Pharisee.

5. You think that increasing personal purity (known as sanctification) can come from anything apart from

> ongoing surrender to Jesus Christ. It's not that we are changing ourselves for God. It's that God changes us when we get out of the way—when we surrender to him. "Partial obedience," observed Oswald Chambers, "is disobedience." Good deeds—deeds that God calls good—are those things that come from the overflow of having been cleansed of all your sins by personal faith in Jesus Christ. When God makes you clean, you begin, by default, to do clean things. This is what Ephesians 2:10 means: "For we are his workmanship, created in Christ Jesus for good works" (ESV). Good works are the overflow of being made good by God himself.

If you put your trust in anything to help you grow in your walk with God apart from surrendering to God and inviting him to finish what he started, you are on your way to becoming a Pharisee.

Great News

The great news is that you can place all your faith in Jesus Christ. God will remove all your sins and make you good in his sight—then your journey of doing good things and being spared from becoming a Pharisee, will begin. But once that journey begins, be careful that you don't allow yourself to go back to your old way of stinking thinking.

> Beware the warning signs of becoming a Pharisee. The danger never goes away. Real repentance, a lifestyle of humble submission to Jesus Christ, is the repellent for the cold, empty, pharisaic way of life.

Notes

Introduction

1. George Orwell quoted in Maria Popova, "Why I Write: George Orwell on an Author's 4 Main Motives," *The Atlantic*, June 25, 2012, https://www.theatlantic.com/entertainment/archive/2012/06/why-i-write-george-orwell-on-an-authors-4-main-motives/258955/.

Chapter 1: Blinders

1. If you haven't yet visited that historic place, make sure it's on your bucket list.
2. Romans 12:1–2: "Therefore, I urge you, brothers and sisters, in view of God's mercy, to offer your bodies as a living sacrifice, holy and pleasing to God—this is your true and proper worship. Do not conform to the pattern of this world, but be transformed by the renewing of your mind. Then you will be able to test and approve what God's will is—his good, pleasing and perfect will."
3. Revelation 7:9.
4. Sabrina Tavernise, "U.S. Suicide Rate Surges to a 30-Year High," *New York Times,* April 22, 2016, https://www.nytimes.com/2016/04/22/health/us-suicide-rate-surges-to-a-30-year-high.html.
5. I highly recommend both of these books by Schaeffer. While intellectually deep, they provide tremendous insight into the root behind the fruit of America's current, growing woes.
6. "Inside a Killer Drug Epidemic: A Look at America's Opioid Crisis," *New York Times,* January 6, 2017, https://www.nytimes.com/2017/01/06/us/opioid-crisis-epidemic.html?_r=0.
7. "14 Shocking Pornography Statistics," United Families International, http://unitedfamilies.org/pornography/14-shocking-pornography-statistics/.
8. Catherine DiBenedetto, "Why Thousands of Women Are Getting

Plastic Surgery Down There," *Health*, March 1, 2017, http://www.health.com/mind-body/why-thousands-of-women-are-getting-plastic-surgery-down-there.

9. Ibid.
10. "41 percent of first marriages end in divorce. 60 percent of second marriages end in divorce. 73 percent of third marriages end in divorce," from "32 Shocking Divorce Statistics," McKinley Irvin Family Law, October 30, 2012, https://www.mckinleyirvin.com/Family-Law-Blog/2012/October/32-Shocking-Divorce-Statistics.aspx.
11. Second Chronicles 7:13–14 is rightly understood to be limited in its application to the theocracy of Israel. America is not a theocracy. Though this passage relates first and foremost to the nation of Israel, the humility of God, and the humility that he looks for among all his people, has not changed. We would do well to not dismiss the importance of repentant humility as an unchanging prerequisite for divine intervention. Divine intervention, in the end, is often sparked by mortals.

Chapter 2: Courage Matters

1. Failure and brokenness can be "back doors" to fulfilling God's objectives in our lives. They position us to listen to him, the necessary prerequisite that must be met before we can do anything for him. The only reason I began preaching on a train station platform was because of personal brokenness and failure that led me, along with Tom (who since then became a best friend) to pray and seek God at 64 Plum Street in New Brunswick, New Jersey. Those times became a pivotal point in my life, and wound up being the very reason I began to speak in public and to preach. I never planned to become a preacher or to enter the world of public speaking. My long-standing goal prior to coming to Christ was to become a criminal trial attorney.
2. Not her real name.
3. Bangers and mash is a tasty dish with sausages and mashed potatoes, magnificently prepared as only the Brits can.
4. To be fair, this man does not accurately reflect the behaviors or attitudes of all Muslims. This is, however, a true story, and the man was indeed a Muslim.
5. Deuteronomy 18:15–22, emphasis added: "The Lord your God will raise up for you *a prophet* like me from among you, from your fellow Israelites. *You must listen to him*. For this is what you asked of the Lord your God at Horeb on the day of the assembly when you said, 'Let us not hear the voice of the Lord our God nor see this great fire anymore, or we will die.' The Lord said to me: 'What they say is good. *I will raise up for them a prophet* like you from among their fellow Israelites, *and I will put my words in his mouth*. He will tell them everything I command him. I myself will call to account anyone who does not listen to my words that the prophet speaks in my name. But a prophet who presumes to speak in my name anything I

have not commanded, or a prophet who speaks in the name of other gods, is to be put to death.' You may say to yourselves, 'How can we know when a message has not been spoken by the LORD?' If what a prophet proclaims in the name of the LORD does not take place or come true, that is a message the LORD has not spoken. That prophet has spoken presumptuously, so do not be alarmed."

Chapter 3: Heroes and Underdogs

1. Read Exodus 33:3 and you will have a deeper appreciation for Moses' plea and passion. He understood that there is no such thing as success without the presence of God.
2. I'm grateful for my friend Jeff Yager who introduced me to this saying.

Chapter 4: Intolerance, the New Tolerance

1. I can't recall if it was Dr. Wayne Dyer, Gary Vaynerchuk, or someone else who first inspired me with this simple parable. I'm thankful it inspired me to create my own way of illustrating it here, and I hope my method proves memorable and helpful to you.
2. It is one thing to be against immigration, which really is xenophobia and perhaps even racist. But it is quite another thing for the people who want to ensure the safety and well-being of those who live in America to be characterized as unreasonable and illogical, which invites nothing more than the undermining of the Constitution, chaos, and eventual anarchy. My grandfather and my great-grandparents were legal immigrants, embracing America and eager to contribute to our nation's success.
3. Not his real name.
4. First John 2:19 warns about false believers among the flock: "They went out from us, but they did not really belong to us. For if they had belonged to us, they would have remained with us; but their going showed that none of them belonged to us." Verse 4 of Jude says, "For certain individuals whose condemnation was written about long ago have secretly slipped in among you. They are ungodly people, who pervert the grace of our God into a license for immorality and deny Jesus Christ our only Sovereign and Lord." The remainder of Jude discloses the dark destiny of wolves in sheep's clothing, and is a sobering reminder for true believers to be on the alert against imposters within the church.
5. Whether Lawrence was ever a believer in the first place, only God knows. My point is that we should always care about and pray for those who are not walking in the truth, and for those who are influenced by their false teaching and conduct.
6. Bitterness is not a small, insignificant sin. Hebrews 12:15 says, "See to it that no one falls short of the grace of God and that no bitter root grows up to cause trouble and defile *many*" (emphasis added).

7. The origin of this quote is debatable, with some attributing it to Edmund Burke. Regardless of its source, its truth is timeless, practical, and incredibly inspiring.

Chapter 5: Resurrecting and Defending Religious Freedom

1. I'm grateful for the tremendous assistance provided by Justin Butterfield, senior counsel and director of Research and Education at First Liberty Institute (www.FirstLiberty.org), for help with this chapter. First Liberty Institute is an excellent organization dedicated to defending religious freedom in America and has compiled an outstanding resource that proves religious freedom in the United States is clearly, and increasingly, under attack. It's called "Undeniable: The Survey of Hostility to Religion in America." It is updated each year, and you can download a free copy by visiting www.FirstLiberty.org. Just type "Undeniable" in the search field and you'll be on your way toward knowing exactly how religion is under attack in the land of the free and the home of the brave.
2. Walsh v. Georgia Dep't of Public Health, No. 1:16-cv-01278 (N.D. Ga., led Apr. 20, 2016). "Undeniable," www.FirstLiberty.org, 2017 edition, 7, 40. To learn more, visit http://www.firstliberty.org/cases/walsh.
3. Ibid.
4. Town of Greece, New York v. Galloway, 134 S. Ct. 1811 (2014), https://www.supremecourt.gov/opinions/13pdf/12–696_bpm1.pdf.
5. "Undeniable," www.FirstLiberty.org, 2017 edition, 13.
6. Town of Greece, New York v. Galloway.
7. See James Hutson, "'A Wall of Separation': FBI Helps Restore Jefferson's Obliterated Draft," Information Bulletin (Library of Congress), 57:6 (June 1998), http://www.loc.gov/loc/lcib/9806/danbury.html. The full text of the relevant paragraph is: "Believing with you that religion is a matter which lies solely between Man & his God, that he owes account to none other for his faith or his worship, that the legitimate powers of government reach actions only, & not opinions, I contemplate with sovereign reverence that act of the whole American people which declared that their legislature should 'make no law respecting an establishment of religion, or prohibiting the free exercise thereof,' thus building a wall of separation between Church & State . . . .Adhering to this expression of the supreme will of the nation in behalf of the rights of conscience, I shall see with friendly dispositions the progress of those sentiments which tend to restore to man all his natural rights, convinced he has no natural rights in opposition to his social duties."
8. The case was decided on May 5, 2014.
9. Mark Hodges, "Christian Could Be Fired for Refusing to Watch LGBT 'Inclusivity' Video," LifeSite, September 15, 2016, https://www

.lifesitenews.com/news/christian-could-lose-his-job-after-refusing-to-watch-lgbt-video.

10. It's always dangerous, and wrong, to paint with such a broad brush that everyone ends up being covered in pigment. This is why I have not done that anwhere in this book. I have focused my attention only on the *radical* or *militant* tactics of people within the LGBTQ community. Not all within that community can be categorized as such. I have met many lesbian, gay, and transgendered people who were nothing but hospitable, humble, and peace-loving. They would not hurt a mosquito, even if infected with the Zika virus. In fact, I have witnessed and experienced a love from a great many people who embrace all sixty-six books of the Bible as the inspired Word of God. A large number of us need to truly repent.
11. In 2013, owners of the Sweetcakes by Melissa bakery, Aaron and Melissa Klein, were approached to make a cake for a same-sex wedding. They felt making a cake for a gay couple would be akin to their celebrating a practice they believe to be against biblical teaching. An Oregon court ruled that the Kleins were discriminating against the couple, violating their civil rights. To be clear, this is not about merely denying a request to bake a cake. The Kleins had made baked goods for this couple in the past. It is about whether or not anyone in America has the right to force the Kleins (who have strong biblical convictions about heterosexual marriage) to celebrate a ceremony that violates what they believe the Bible teaches. This distinction is crucial to understanding the case and the application of the First Amendment. The Kleins did not stand in the way of the lesbian couple's marriage. The lesbian couple, however, sought to compel the Kleins to celebrate their union. In America, is it just to compel someone to celebrate something that they feel violates their religious beliefs? In December 2015, the Kleins paid the fine, with interest, but the financial strain was too much, forcing them to shut down their bakery and to lose their livelihood. The Kleins made a public statement about the case after the oral arguments were made, which I urge you to watch, here: https://www.facebook.com/firstlibertyinstitute/videos/10155134357719673.
12. "Masterpiece Cakeshop v. Colorado Civil Rights Commission," Alliance Defending Freedom, September 8, 2017, http://www.adfmedia.org/news/prdetail/8700; the Supreme Court petition can be found at http://www.adfmedia.org/files/MasterpieceCertPetition.pdf.
13. "Colo. Cake Artist Weighing All Options After State High Court Declines to Take Case," Alliance Defending Freedom, April 25, 2016, www.adfmedia.org/News/PRDetail/9936.
14. "Colorado Cake Artist Asks US Supreme Court to Protect His Freedom of Expression," Alliance Defending Freedom, July 22, 2016, https://www.adflegal.org/detailspages/press-release-details/colorado-cake-artist-asks-us-supreme-court-to-protect-his-freedom-of-expression.

15. Ibid.
16. Here I am again emphasizing the importance of this distinction. I am referring to those within the LGBTQ community who have mastered the art of reverse intolerance, those who seek to destroy the views of anyone who disagrees with them.
17. These are the words Ravenhill wrote me in a personal letter, which I still have to this day.
18. "Coach Kennedy," First Liberty, http://firstliberty.org/cases/coachkennedy/.
19. Kennedy v. Bremerton School District, No. 16–35801, https://firstliberty.org/cases/coachkennedy/; "Undeniable," www.FirstLiberty.org, 2017 edition, 15, 232. You can read Coach Kennedy's perspective at https://firstliberty.org/wp-content/uploads/2016/01/Kennedy-EEOC-Intake-Questionnaire-and-Supporting-Materials_Redacted.pdf.
20. "Walt Tutka," First Liberty, http://www.firstliberty.org/cases/tutka.
21. "Undeniable," www.FirstLiberty.org, 2017 edition, 16, 286.
22. "Opulent Life Church," First Liberty, http://firstliberty.org/cases/opulentlifechurch/. You can read the church's brief before the Fifth Circuit Court at https://firstliberty.org/wp-content/uploads/2016/03/Opulent-Life-Brief-for-Appellants.pdf.
23. Ibid., 18, 324.
24. Ibid., 18, 357.
25. Eric Nicholson, "Liberty Institute Helps Dallas Orthodox Synagogue Defeat Neighbors' Attempt to Close It," *Dallas Observer*, Frebruary 5, 2015, http://www.dallasobserver.com/news/liberty-institute-helps-dallas-orthodox-synagogue-defeat-neighbors-attempt-to-close-it-7127264; Eric Nicholson, "After Years of Wandering, a Dallas Synagogue Find a Home—and a Chilly Welcome," *Dallas Observer*, April 30, 2015, http://www.dallasobserver.com/news/after-years-of-wandering-a-dallas-synagogue-finds-a-home-and-a-chilly-welcome-7182328.
26. "Chaplain Modder," First Liberty, http://firstliberty.org/cases/chaplainmodde. "Undeniable," www.FirstLiberty.org, 2017 edition, 20, 402. The Bible teaches that sexual activity outside the confines of marriage is wrong, even if between heterosexuals. Singling out same-sex sexual activity is an incomplete portrayal of sexual sin.
27. "Air Force Veteran Persecuted for Religious Beliefs," First Liberty, http://firstliberty.org/cases/monk/.
28. Ibid.
29. Unfortunately, some churches and religious organizations have tolerated heterosexual sin while taking a hard line on homosexual sin. On the surface this imbalanced approach looks like an attempt to follow their religious beliefs, while they actually end up looking like they are engaging in anti-LGBTQ discrimination. And such an inconsistent application of Scripture also weakens their legal options.

Chapter 6: Speaking Truth with Love

1. Not their real names.
2. Many of the lessons I've learned in life, I've learned through failure. Sadly, I have been sexually immoral in my past, having done and said things that are clearly prohibited in the Bible. I'm not proud of doing so, and I share my guilt—as well as the forgiveness I've received through Christ—to encourage anyone who has a sordid past. Jesus offers genuine forgiveness to anyone who truly repents. If sharing from my failures helps others succeed, I am happy to do so.
3. Any and all sexual immorality can be forgiven—if one sincerely repents and asks God, through Christ, for forgiveness. First John 1:9 says, "If we confess our sins, he is faithful and just and will forgive us our sins and purify us from all unrighteousness." This book is not intended to exhaust all the possible forms of *pornea*, sexual immorality. Viewing pornography, for instance, is also a form of sexual immorality.
4. Peter, you may recall, denied Jesus completely, three times—even after being warned in advance that he would do so. If God can use Peter, he can use anyone.
5. Despite our discussion, Devin and Mark went on to adopt the children. They even called to tell us the news, because they knew that even though we had different views of parenting, our love for each other would remain unshakable.
6. Matthew 11:19; Luke 7:34.
7. John and Gina are not their real names.

Chapter 7: Did Jesus Judge?

1. This statement may also be attributed to D. L. Moody.
2. Paul discussed his weaknesses of the flesh in 2 Corinthians 11:29, and his murderous, violent, blasphemous past in 1 Timothy 1:13–14.

Chapter 8: The Present Future

1. I also think it's good to listen to every sermon as if it were the last one you'll hear, and to pay attention to each reading of the Bible as if it were your last chance to read it. A sense of urgency to apply God's Word will revolutionize your life.
2. I'm not sure we should be about going back to some nebulous idea of greatness for America but rather about going ahead, to become a nation that is better than ever.
3. By "hail Mary," I mean as in football, not prayer.
4. Comments delivered by Democratic presidential candidate Hillary Clinton on April 23, 2015, at the Women in the World Summit in New York City. https://votesmart.org/public-statement/994018/women-in-the-world-summit-2015-keynote-address#.WcvNm9OGP5Y.

5. Italics emphasis mine.
6. Italics emphasis mine.
7. Italics emphasis mine.
8. *Fugazy* is Italian slang for *fake.*

Chapter 9: Broken Glass

1. "1938: The Night of Broken Glass," History.com, http://www.history.com/this-day-in-history/the-night-of-broken-glass; "The 'Night of Broken Glass,'" United States Holocaust Memorial Museum, https://www.ushmm.org/outreach/en/article.php?ModuleId=10007697.
2. "In Today's Economy, Even Two-Income Families Struggle to Make Ends Meet," PBS Newshour, June 10, 2016, http://www.pbs.org/newshour/bb/in-todays-economy-even-two-income-families-struggle-to-make-ends-meet/.
3. Kelly Wallace, "Teens Spend a 'Mind-Boggling' 9 Hours a Day Using Media, Report Says," CNN, November 3, 2015, http://www.cnn.com/2015/11/03/health/teens-tweens-media-screen-use-repor/; Jacqueline Howard, "Americans Devote More Than 10 Hours a Day to Screen Time, and Growing," CNN, July 29, 2016, http://www.cnn.com/2016/06/30/health/americans-screen-time-nielsen/; Madlen Davies, "Average Person Now Spends More Time on Their Phone and Laptop Than SLEEPING, Study Claims," DailyMail.com, March 11, 2015, http://www.dailymail.co.uk/health/article-2989952/How-technology-taking-lives-spend-time-phones-laptops-SLEEPING.html.
4. George Santayana, *The Life of Reason: Reason in Common Sense* (New York: Scribner's, 1905), 284.
5. Winston Churchill, "Air Parity Lost," speech to the House of Commons, May 2, 1935, https://www.winstonchurchill.org/resources/speeches/1930–1938-the-wilderness/air-parity-lost.
6. Certainly, anyone could make an accusation. But likening any American president to Adolf Hitler at this time in our history has yet to be substantiated by parallel acts of atrocity.
7. The exact origin of this poem is historically uncertain, but the earliest known version of the rhyme is found in John Gower's *Confesio Amantis* (1390).
8. S.1857—National Defense Authorization Act for Fiscal Year 2012, 112th Congress, www.gpo.gov.fdsys/pkg/PLAW-112pub181/pdf/PLAW-112publ181.pdf, 267.
9. "NDAA Sections 1021 and 1022: Scary Potential," Tenth Amendment Center, http://tenthamendmentcenter.com/2012/02/06/ndaa-sections-1021-and-1022-scary-potential/; "Indefinite Detention, Endless Worldwide War and the 2012 National Defense Authorization Act," ACLU, https://www.aclu.org/feature/indefinite-detention-endless-worldwide-war-and-2012-national-defense-authorization-act; "National Defense Authorization Act for Fiscal Year 2012," Wikipedia, https://en.wikipedia.org/wiki

/National_Defense_Authorization_Act_for_Fiscal_Year_2012; "National Defense Authorization Act," Snopes, http://www.snopes.com/politics/military/ndaa.asp; "Sections 1021, 1022 of NDAA," Montgomery County Civil Rights Coalition, https://mococivilrights.wordpress.com/campaigns/ndaa/mccrc-ndaaaumf-resolution/sections-1021–1022-of-ndaa/.

10. H.R. 1540 (112th): National Defense Authorization Act for Fiscal Year 2012, GovTrack: https://www.GovTrack.us/congress/bills/112/hr1540/text.
11. Ibid.
12. "Sen. Rand Paul Objects to Indefinite Detention Language in NDAA," YouTube, December 21, 2012, video, 8:44, https://www.youtube.com/watch?v=GvuhVu0z9p4; Naomi Wolf, "The NDAA: A Clear and Present Danger to American Liberty," *The Guardian*, February 29, 2012, https://www.theguardian.com/commentisfree/cifamerica/2012/feb/29/ndaa-danger-american-liberty; "President Obama Signs Indefinite Detention Bill into Law," ACLU, December 31, 2011, https://www.aclu.org/news/president-obama-signs-indefinite-detention-bill-law; Even Snopes.com cannot easily put the matter to rest, "National Defense Authorization Act," Snopes, January 2, 2012, http://www.snopes.com/politics/military/ndaa.asp.
13. Mark Knoller, "Obama Signs Defense Bill, with 'Reservations,'" CBSNews, January 1, 2012, http://www.cbsnews.com/news/obama-signs-defense-bill-with-reservations/.
14. Ibid.
15. The Sixth Amendment to the Constitution provides for a fair and speedy trial: "In all criminal prosecutions, the accused shall enjoy the right to a speedy and public trial, by an impartial jury of the State and district wherein the crime shall have been committed, which district shall have been previously ascertained by law, and to be informed of the nature and cause of the accusation; to be confronted with the witnesses against him; to have compulsory process for obtaining witnesses in his favor, and to have the Assistance of Counsel for his defence."
16. Mark Knoller, "Obama Signs Defense Bill, with 'Reservations,'" CBSNews, January 1, 2012, http://www.cbsnews.com/news/obama-signs-defense-bill-with-reservations/.
17. "Indefinite Detention, Endless Worldwide War and the 2012 National Defense Authorization Act," ACLU, https://www.aclu.org/feature/indefinite-detention-endless-worldwide-war-and-2012-national-defense-authorization-act; Christopher Anders, "A Slick Trick on the NDAA and Indefinite Detention; Don't Be Fooled!" ACLU, April 19, 2012, https://www.aclu.org/blog/slick-trick-ndaa-and-indefinite-detention-dont-be-fooled.
18. *The Heritage Guide to the Constitution,* The Heritage Foundation, http://www.heritage.org/constitution/#!/constitution#essay-61.
19. The Sixth Amendment guarantees the right to a speedy trial and the Fourteenth Amendment guarantees due process.

20. "Congressman Scott Perry," US House of Rep, https://perry.house.gov/.
21. "Perry Named Chairman of Homeland Security Subcommittee," Congressman Scott Perry, January 5, 2015, http://perry.house.gov/news/documentsingle.aspx?DocumentID=398024.
22. "Homeland Security Aims to Buy 1.6 Billion Rounds of Ammo," *Denver Post,* February 14, 2013, http://www.denverpost.com/2013/02/14/homeland-security-aims-to-buy-1–6-billion-rounds-of-ammo/; Ralph Benko, "1.6 Billion Rounds of Ammo for Homeland Security? It's Time for a National Conversation," *Forbes,* March 11, 2013, http://www.forbes.com/sites/ralphbenko/2013/03/11/1–6-billion-rounds-of-ammo-for-homeland-security-its-time-for-a-national-conversation/#25e5f9c05e01.
23. Andrew Buncombe, "US Forced to Import Bullets from Israel as Troops Use 250,000 for Every Rebel Killed," *Belfast Telegraph,* January 10, 2011, http://www.belfasttelegraph.co.uk/news/world-news/us-forced-to-import-bullets-from-israel-as-troops-use-250000-for-every-rebel-killed-28580666.html.
24. Article 1, Section viii, Clause xii, http://www.heritage.org/constitution/#!/constitution#essay-52.
25. Adam Andrzejewski, "War Weapons for America's Police Departments: New Data Shows Feds Transfer $2.2B in Military Gear," *Forbes,* May 10, 2016, http://www.forbes.com/sites/adamandrzejewski/2016/05/10/war-weapons-for-americas-local-police-departments/#4afaba4b54fe.
26. Ibid.
27. Eyder Peralta and David Eads, "White House Ban on Militarized Gear for Police May Mean Little," *The Two-way: Breaking News from NPR,* May 21, 2015, http://www.npr.org/sections/thetwo-way/2015/05/21/407958035/white-house-ban-on-militarized-gear-for-police-may-mean-little.
28. Ibid.
29. Ibid.
30. Ibid.
31. Ibid.
32. "Cougar 4x4 MRAP," Military.com, http://www.military.com/equipment/cougar-4x4-mrap, accessed October 2, 2017.
33. Article 1, Section viii, Clause xii, http://www.heritage.org/constitution/#!/constitution#essay-52.
34. David Kessler, "The 5 Stages of Grief: A Message from David Kessler." Grief.com, https://grief.com/the-five-stages-of-grief/.

Chapter 10: How to Handle Racists, #Haters—and Many Folks In Between

1. Attempting to address all possible scenarios would take volumes to exhaust. These are provided to identify the most obvious situations that you may come across.

2. Mormons, while part of what they call "The Church of Jesus Christ of Latter-day Saints," do not believe many of the same, fundamental things embraced by Orthodox, historic Christianity. Did you know, for instance, that they believe Satan is Jesus' spirit-brother, and many other things that are heretical and clearly against what the Bible teaches? For more information, visit Tyler O'Neil, "Ex-Mormon Shares Secrets from the Church of Latter-day Saints." *Christian Post*, August 19, 2013, http://www.christianpost.com/news/ex-mormon-shares-secrets-from-the-church-of-latter-day-saints-102588/; Loren Franck, "Ten Lies I Told As a Mormon Missionary," Mormonism Research Ministry, http://www.mrm.org/ten-lies; Don Koenig, "Doctrines of the Latter-day Saints of Deception," The Prophetic Years, http://www.thepropheticyears.com/cults/mormons.HTM; Ken Clark, "LDS Honesty: Lying for the Lord," Mormon Think, http://www.mormonthink.com/lying.htm; Valerie Tarico and Tony Nugent, "Twelve Beliefs the Mormon Church Might Not Want You to Know About." ValerieTarico.com, October 5, 2012, https://valerietarico.com/2012/10/05/the-same-god-twelve-beliefs-mormons-might-not-want-you-to-know-about/.
3. Matthew 7:6 NKJV.
4. Matthew 13:24–30.
5. Suet is the fat found around the hips and haunches of cows and lambs. It also refers to a mixture of fat or peanut butter and bird seed and is often used to feed birds in the winter. Chickadees, jays, starlings, and woodpeckers find it especially tasty. Try putting some out for your feathered friends, and they'll love you for it.
6. For more self-analysis on whether you may be a well-meaning, unintentional hypocrite, make sure you check out the appendix, "Ten Signs You May Be Morphing into a Pharisee." The number one thing pastors and Christian leaders must be doing is guarding their own hearts and lives (watching their lives and doctrine closely, as 1 Timothy 4:16 warns), so they truly walk with God. Then, and only then, can they help their people sojourn with the Sovereign.
7. Emphasis added.

Chapter 11: Secret Weapons

1. "P.J. O'Rourke," Wikiquote, https://en.wikiquote.org/wiki/P._J._O%27Rourke, last updated Aug. 5, 2017.
2. Italics, emphasis mine.
3. I encourage you to read the Bible with an eye open for all the times God makes a conditional promise to bless us. There are thousands of places in the Bible where God's blessings require human obedience.
4. The word *resistance* has been branded to mean something very different in America in 2017 than I mean it here. Here, I am not referring to resistance

as #theresistance has come to use it. I mean it in the sense of resisting anything and everything that opposes biblical truth, the glory of God, and our Constitution.

5. Kelly Wallace, "Teens Spend a 'Mind-Boggling' 9 Hours a Day Using Media, Report Says," CNN, November 3, 2015, http://www.cnn.com/2015/11/03/health/teens-tweens-media-screen-use-report/; Jacqueline Howard, "Americans Devote More Than 10 Hours a Day to Screen Time, and Growing," CNN, July 29, 2016, http://www.cnn.com/2016/06/30/health/americans-screen-time-nielsen/; Madlen Davies, "Average Person Now Spends More Time on Their Phone and Laptop Than SLEEPING, Study Claims," DailyMail.com, March 11, 2015, http://www.dailymail.co.uk/health/article-2989952/How-technology-taking-lives-spend-time-phones-laptops-SLEEPING.html.
6. Romans 12:1–2 is a powerful command, not a suggestion, to reject thinking and living the way the world wants us to and to embrace our transformation—beginning with our minds.
7. Samuel Greengard, "Are We Losing Our Ability to Think Critically?," *Communications of the ACM*, 2009, 52(7), 18–19, http://cacm.acm.org/magazines/2009/7/32082-are-we-losing-our-ability-to-think-critically/fulltext.
8. Ibid.
9. Ibid.
10. Ibid.
11. Ibid.
12. Ibid.
13. Ibid.
14. Stuart Wolpert, "In Our Digital World, Are Young People Losing the Ability to Read Emotions?," UCLA Newsroom, August 21, 2014, http://newsroom.ucla.edu/releases/in-our-digital-world-are-young-people-losing-the-ability-to-read-emotions.
15. Amy Morin, "Is Technology Ruining Our Ability to Read Emotions? Study Says Yes," *Forbes,* August 26, 2014, https://www.forbes.com/sites/amymorin/2014/08/26/is-technology-ruining-our-ability-to-read-emotions-study-says-yes/#1dee8ef246a5.
16. Emphasis added.
17. Emphasis added.
18. Visit our store at CourageMatters.com, and you'll find great resources to help you embrace repentance as a lifestyle. But that's not all. You'll find resources that will help you in every area of life.
19. See Matthew 7:3–5 and Luke 6:42. Note that Jesus did not say we should never address a sin in the life of another person. He said that we should first make sure we are addressing the sins in our own lives.

Chapter 12: Battle Plan

1. 1 Peter 1:22.
2. Gene Kranz was the *Apollo 13* flight director. On the fateful night of April 13, 1970, hopes of landing on the moon were lost after an explosion threatened the lives of the crew—who, against incredible adversity, returned home to earth safe and sound on April 17. It is the resolve of men and women like Kranz that is needed in today's adverse circumstances. "Failure is Not an Option," NASA, September 30, 2011, https://www.nasa.gov/multimedia/imagegallery/image_feature_2073.html.
3. "Minority Rules: Scientists Discover Tipping Point for the Spread of Ideas," RPI News, Rensselaer, July 25, 2011, https://news.rpi.edu/luwakkey/2902.
4. Quoted by Amy Rees Anderson, "'Resentment Is Like Taking Poison and Waiting for the Other Person to Die.'" *Forbes*, April 7, 2015, https://www.forbes.com/sites/amyanderson/2015/04/07/resentment-is-like-taking-poison-and-waiting-for-the-other-person-to-die/#1a19dd23446c.
5. "To err is human, to forgive is divine," is from "An Essay on Criticism," by Alexander Pope.
6. Just be careful, in the process, that you don't condone the sin or participate in it. Jesus, again, sets our example.

Chapter 13: Awakening the Sleeping Giant

1. Erin Bradrick, "Churches and Political Activity: The Call to Repeal the Johnson Amendment," NPQ, July 27, 2016, https://nonprofitquarterly.org/2016/07/27/churches-political-activity-call-repeal-johnson-amendment; C. Eugene Emery Jr., "Donald Trump Correct—Lyndon Johnson Passed Legislation Limiting Political Activity of Churches," *PolitiFact*, July 22, 2016, http://www.politifact.com/truth-o-meter/statements/2016/jul/22/donald-trump/donald-trump-correct-lyndon-johnson-passed-legisla/.
2. *The Heritage Guide to the Constitution*, The Heritage Foundation, http://www.heritage.org/constitution/#!/articles/2/essays/85/oath-of-office.

Suggested Reading List and Resources

I'm a firm believer that the Bible is the Word of God, unlike any other book written and compiled. By providing this list of other books and organizations, I'm not endorsing everything presented by each. I encourage you to use your discretion, think deeply, and respond accordingly.

Books to Help Improve Communication and Relationship Skills

- The Bible: I'm often asked which version of the Bible is best. My answer is simple: the one you read and apply.
- *Living by the Book: The Art and Science of Reading the Bible* by Howard G. Hendricks and William D. Hendricks, Moody Publishers
- *How to Read the Bible for All Its Worth* by Gordon Fee and Douglas Stewart, Zondervan
- *How to Win Friends and Influence People* by Dale Carnegie

SUGGESTED READING AND RESOURCES

Books to Help Understand Tyranny and Oppression

- *1984* by George Orwell
- *Animal Farm* by George Orwell

Websites About the Constitution and Freedom

First Liberty Institute: FirstLiberty.org
The Heritage Association: Heritage.org
Alliance for Defending Freedom: ADFLegal.org

About the Author

"Life is too short to pursue anything less than your passion," says Michael Anthony Paolicelli (pal-uh-*chell*-ee), who goes by his first and middle names for simplicity's sake.

And he should know—his life to date has been marked by serious adversity, including multiple brushes with death, a battle with cancer, surviving several kidnapping/luring attempts as a child, and being estranged from his father for many years before an amazing reconciliation.

These challenges have helped Michael inspire, challenge, and motivate people around the world to think deeply, to live courageously, and to squeeze every drop out of life, which he does through his work as an award-winning speaker, author, and blogger. If you're looking for someone to ignite your people with humble courage, reach out to Michael.

Michael is regularly featured in major publications and news outlets around the world, as well as on his own website CourageMatters.com and the free *Courage Matters*™ app, where he helps people discover, develop, and live with courage in every area of life.

Hailed as a "modern-day Jonathan Edwards," Michael has been

called an "extraordinary" communicator with a "teachable" and "humble spirit," noted for his eloquence and the rare combination of a passionate, prophetic voice and a genuinely humble approach to dialogue. Listening to or watching him communicate is always engaging, enlightening, and inspiring.

Michael began public speaking on a train station platform in New Brunswick, New Jersey, the result of deep personal trauma that nearly undid him. That laid the groundwork for what would become a career communicating to diverse crowds around the world, in more than twenty countries, on four continents. His *Godfactor*® radio broadcast in the United States has a potential listener audience of two to three million people.

He and his wife, Janet, are cofounders of The National Week of Repentance™, and Godfactor®, Inc., a nonprofit ministry that helps people discover and enjoy God with podcasts, videos, and written resources. If you appreciate solid, practical Bible teaching, you'll love Godfactor.com.

Michael is an ordained minister and received his BA in English from Rutgers University. He is a graduate of Moody Graduate School in Chicago (ASP) and Multnomah Biblical Seminary in Portland, Oregon (MDiv).

He is passionate about helping people live lives worthy of replication and attributes most of the lessons he's learned in life to adversity. He loves comedy, music, international travel, and experiencing new cultures.

Michael adores his wife, Janet, and their two sons, Titus and Simeon. His greatest pleasure in all of life is spending time with them any way he can.

Connect with

MICHAEL ANTHONY

For Speaking Invitations, Interview Requests, and Social Media:

CourageMatters.com

The Courage Matters™ app

CPSIA information can be obtained
at www.ICGtesting.com
Printed in the USA
LVHW031204040523
746114LV00006B/37

9 781400 247431